STORY WORKSHOP
New Possibilities for Young Writers

Susan Harris MacKay

with Kerry Salazar
and Opal School Teacher Researchers

STORY WORKSHOP
New Possibilities for Young Writers

HEINEMANN
Portsmouth, NH

Heinemann

361 Hanover Street

Portsmouth, NH 03801–3912

www.heinemann.com

Offices and agents throughout the world

The author and publisher wish to thank those who have generously given permission to reprint borrowed material:

Bulleted list from *Write from the Start* by Donald Graves and Virginia Stuart. Copyright © 1985 by Donald H. Graves and Virginia Stuart. Used by permission of Dutton, an imprint of Penguin Publishing Group, a division of Penguin Random House LLC.

Figure 6.1 illustrated by David Huyck, in consultation with Sarah Park Dohlen, from blog entry "Picture This: Diversity in Children's Books 2018 Infographic" by Sarah Park Dahlen, posted June 19, 2019 on sarahpark.com. Used by permission of the illustrator.

Library of Congress Control Number: 2021931444

ISBN: 978-0-325-12034-8

Editor: Zoë Ryder White
Production Editors: Kimberly Capriola, Sonja Chapman
Cover and Interior Designer: Monica Ann Cohen
Typesetter: Gina Poirier, Gina Poirier Design
Manufacturing: Val Cooper
Video Production and Editing: Kathryn Ann Myers

Printed in the United States of America on acid-free paper
1   2   3   4   5   VP   25   24   23   22   21
February 2021 Printing

Max and I enjoy a family story.

CONTENTS

VIDEO CONTENTS

See the following page for directions on how to access the videos and online resources.

ONLINE RESOURCE CONTENTS

How to Access Videos and Online Resources

To access the Online Resources and videos for *Story Workshop*:

1. Go to **http://hein.pub/StoryWorkshop-login**.

2. Log in with your username and password. If you do not already have an account with Heinemann, you will need to create an account.

3. On the Welcome page, choose "Click here to register an Online Resource."

4. Register your product by entering the code: **STORYWS** (be sure to read and check the acknowledgment box under the keycode).

5. Once you have registered your product, it will appear alphabetically in your account list of My Online Resources.

Note: When returning to Heinemann.com to access your previously registered products, simply log into your Heinemann account and click on "View my registered Online Resources."

ACKNOWLEDGMENTS

Story workshop emerged from a laboratory of teacher research called Opal School. Since 2001, it has been a tiny school with a big mission: to strengthen education through provoking fresh ideas concerning environments where creativity, imagination, and the wonder of learning thrive. This book is one way Opal School pursued that mission and is the result of nearly two decades of collaborative research. I am eternally grateful for the opportunity to have been part of this effort and to have received support and counsel from wise colleagues—whose work had great influence on Opal School and on my thinking—such as Louise Cadwell, Ben Mardell, Mara Krechevsky, Tiziana Fillipini, and Lella Gandini. Caroline Wolfe was the first person generous enough to invite me into the work at Opal School, as she and a team, including Judy Graves, were developing it. I was thrilled to join them, Erin Moulton, Tara Papandrew, and Marni Gardner soon after. Nicole Simpson-Tanner, Mary Gage Davis, and Kimie Fukuda arrived around the time that Judy, Opal's founding director, asked the question, "What is the relationship between literacy and the arts?" And story workshop began with Josephine, Scouten, Tseten, Jaden, Max, Bradford, Bryanna, Liam, Sydney, Maya, Emmerson, Aiden, Anna, Elke, Keali'i, and Ross, who are all young adults by now. Not too long after, Kerry Salazar, Joey Hewitt, Amy Maki, Zalika Gardner, Steve Davee, Marcy Berkowitz, Levia Friedman, Sierra Freeman, Hannah Chandler, Kathryn Ann Myers, Lauren Adams, Carole Burton, and Matt Karlsen came along to help. Parents such as Carolyn Johnson-Evans, Beth Hutchins, and Paula Dion supported the school as volunteers and then continued as staff as their children grew. New teachers arrived and extended the research. Among them were Heather Scerba, Xavier Pierce, Leslie Bachman, Hana Hutchings, Colesie Tharp, Kye Ginger, Katharine Anderson, Chris Varley, and Sarah MacPherson. All of them and more have had a hand in developing what we understand about the power of the arts and play and their relationship to literacy. This project has benefitted tremendously from the research of other teachers who have been developing their own story workshop practices. In these pages, you'll meet a few of them.

Images throughout the book come from Opal School, as well as other schools: Prescott, Annieville Kinders, and High Tech Elementary. This book would not have been possible without this collective effort. It would not have happened without Zoë Ryder White's determination to support us in finding the beginning of what we had to say and share, or without Matt Glover's introduction and encouragement. It would not have happened without Zoë's kind, patient, supportive, imaginative, and pragmatic vision for what could be. Working with Zoë has been among the most delightful, enjoyable, and encouraging parts of this process. I'm grateful for the whole team at Heinemann who believed in this project and have supported it all along the way. Thank you: Roderick Spelman, Sarah Fournier, Catrina Swasey, Patty Adams, Kimberly Capriola, Sonja Chapman, Monica Cohen, Jillian Sims, Kimberly Cahill, and Val Cooper. Kathryn Ann is the beautiful and creative vision behind the videos that make this project come alive. Ever generous with enthusiasm and good ideas, Kathryn Ann was a major contributor to this process. Sherry Day and Paul Tomasyan from Heinemann were a tremendous support to the video process, and we were delighted to have them with us in Portland for guidance, good advice, and good food.

Charlotte Karlsen—who graduated from Opal School many years before she graduated this year, pandemic-style, from Bates College—proofread the Works Cited, and I am grateful for her expert eyes. Her father, Matt, a long-time friend and colleague, held this thing together. His gifts of facilitation, problem solving, listening, organization, imagination, questioning, synthesis, courage, and collaboration have left their marks all over this project in the ways that remain frustratingly invisible in the end, but without which we would have had nothing—or, at least, nothing that would have mattered nearly as much.

Kerry, my story workshop partner for many years, wrote tool after tool and interviewed Aeriale, Melinda, Shelby, Rosemarie, and Alana, who were so generous with their time. She did this while working directly with children and teachers, and while waiting for Cecelia to arrive, whom we finally welcomed to the world with great hope and love. I'm so grateful I've had the chance to develop this big idea with her and for her unending optimism, compassionate leadership, and light-up-the-room smile.

And then there's my beloved family—Bob, Sophie, Max, and Stella—who would want me to mention the dogs—Lucy and Maisie—who, in fairness, were my most steadfast writing companions. There's no this (book or school) without them. My children are Opal School graduates, and I've had the benefit of witnessing the seeds planted there grow and bloom in stunningly beautiful ways. But I need to acknowledge Max in particular, at this moment, for what he has taught me about stories and how we live not only with them but through them, because of them. As I wrote this book, Max spent his nineteenth year working on many important things, one of which was fighting metastatic testicular cancer. It has been an arduous, unspeakably painful journey that provided the accompaniment to the writing of this book and that has deepened my appreciation for the power of story in ways I never could have imagined.

As this project wrapped, the planet was in crisis, our cities were burning, people all over the world were battling a pandemic, depression loomed, and my son was in cancer treatment. Thirteen-year-old Stella said recently, tearful and bewildered, "You don't know what's going to happen. You never know what's going to happen. You don't." It was a cry of frustration at the universe and the uncertainty we live with every moment, but it was also a revelation, filled with awe at the expanse of the possibility of everything. "You guys," she told us, "You. Don't. Ever. Know."

The stories we tell allow us to recognize just how endlessly wide and narrowly defined possibility can be at the very same time. Stories are ballast as we turn blind corners around this often-terrifying terrain. The stories we know, the more we tell them, and the intention with which we craft them make the world in which we live together. Based on the stories we've already lived, felt, heard, and imagined, our brains continually predict things we cannot know and insist we know them anyway. So, as we're overwhelmed by what's wrong, what we *can* do is commit to feeling more, listening more, and imagining more. If we can stay awake, the stories we have to tell are in our control. Let's craft the stories of today that will most likely help us tell the ones we want to live in tomorrow. Max taught me this. I am indebted to his courage, his imagination, his strength, and his story.

PRELUDE

While I am working with another child, I'm suddenly intrigued by what Scouten is doing across the room. In this kindergarten and first-grade classroom, there is a small space between an easel and a bookcase, just big enough for a six-year-old person to turn around. Scouten has found that space to be a convenient location for her to create during story workshop because the bookshelf allows her a spot to place both the tape recorder that will play her music and the clipboard that holds the paper where she'll capture her writing. The space in between gives her the room she needs to dance her way into her story.

I watch her press Play and move to the soft music; then she presses Stop, picks up her pencil, and writes. And then again, and again, until she comes to me, breathless and excited, to read what she has written.

But I'm too impatient to listen to the story. I want to know more about her process and so I ask her to tell me that first. "Scouten, tell me about what you were doing to write that story!"

Scouten looks at me somewhat impatiently but answers, "I started dancing it out and I picked out a song and I wondered what I should do for both the birds and the flowers. But it worked out." And she looks at me intently enough to snap me out of my fascination with how she created her story—and instead listen to her story!

She reads, "First the birds are singing and eating the seeds from the flower. Sang Miss Bird, 'The sky is getting dark.' It began to rain. 'Quickly, go in our nest.' The flowers said, 'Be safe.' And instead of blooming, they started going backwards. When the rain stopped, the flower came up slowly making sure no one was going to pounce on it. Then the bird came out slowly making sure that no hunter was near."

"Wow, Scouten!" I say. "What an exciting story. I love the repetitive language you've used at the end." And, not to be deterred, I add, "How did you come up with that?"

This time, Scouten says nothing but jumps out of her chair and dances a piece of her dance.

Welcome to story workshop. I'm so glad you've stepped into this joyful place to learn alongside children and the many colleagues you'll find, working to make sense of new possibilities to reinvigorate old commitments that support these beliefs and values:

- Children have a right to write.

- Children want to write.

- Children's writing is a way of saying, "Here I am."

- When children's writing is central to the life of a community of classroom authors, it creates the opportunity for each child to realize "I matter."

- When children have the opportunity to practice daily the skills and strategies that allow them to exercise their rights to belong in a community where everyone else has the same rights, the result is an indelible sense of agency and empathy that the health of our democracy relies on to survive.

Let's get started!

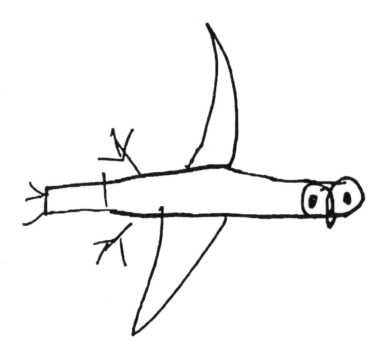

INTRODUCTION

Story workshop started with a question embraced by teacher-researchers at Opal School, including me and my colleagues. We asked: *What is the connection between literacy and the arts?* Inspired and curious about the rich landscape we expected to find around this intersection, we asked more questions:

- What might be the role of play?

- What happens when we infuse writing workshop with ample use of the arts and time to play?

- How do the voice and the choice that result when we invite children to create and tell their stories lead a classroom to practice the habits of healthy democracy?

- How does this practice, as a first priority, both rely on and reinforce equity and access for all?

Years before I arrived at Opal School, I had become a teacher because I had discovered writing workshop. I didn't expect to want to be a teacher. But when I was a sophomore at Vassar College, I did want to earn the credit available to me if I did some fieldwork off-site and got out of my college classrooms. I signed up to volunteer in a Poughkeepsie public elementary school and was assigned an advisor from Vassar's education department. Who assigned me some books to read. Which annoyed me. I thought that the fieldwork option would be a break from the books. I was so tired of the tedium of my own schooling. But to my great surprise—utter astonishment, really—when I opened the first book, Donald Graves and Virginia Stuart's *Write from the Start: Tapping Your Child's Natural Writing Ability* (1985), which had been published only a few years earlier, I was hooked by page 18. I have such a strong memory of me, lying on my bed in my dorm room, reluctantly opening this book, fully expecting to die of boredom. But instead, I was thrilled, inspired, and literally filled with a new life purpose, which I think is what people

Stories tell you what the truth is. Stories tell you what to believe and tell you how to believe. Stories become a part of you after you listen to them. Stories help you believe.

—Sutton (age 9)

mean when they say they found their calling. Here is some of what I found there that lit the fire that still burns in me:

> Our greatest problem is that we underestimate what children can do. We underestimate their will to make sense of themselves and the world around them. Children are curious and want their curiosity satisfied. But we don't know children, nor the interests that arouse their curiosity, nor the learning process well enough to know how to respond to them. We constantly try to trick them into learning things that have nothing to do with them. Most of our classrooms are reflections of what teachers do, not of what children do. If our classrooms are to be effective, they should be filled with stuff, the stuff of what children know and what they want to know more about. (Graves and Stuart 1985, 18)

Story workshop creates a platform for schools to see the will children have to make sense of themselves and their world. Children are invited to satisfy their curiosity and adults see more clearly that they are bursting with it. As story workshops ignite in classrooms around the world, teachers shift classrooms to reflect the children who inhabit them. Story workshop invites teachers who understand that children learn best through play, but struggle to find a place for it, to infuse it right into literacy instructional time—and they are seeing the explosion of motivation and engagement that happens when they do. Story workshop helps teachers who have practiced writing workshop for a long time, but have been challenged by those students who say they never have anything to write about, find out that all children have stories to tell. Story workshop allows teachers who lament the loss of the arts in the child's school day to find a way to put them to use in new ways that work for everyone.

Though a copy of *Write from the Start* has always been on my bookshelf, I hadn't opened it for over twenty-five years until I was preparing to write this book. For the last eighteen of those years, I've been working at Opal School in Portland, Oregon. Opal School serves 125 three- to eleven-year-old children and their families as well as thousands of educators each year who attend professional development workshops in person or online. Opal was started because the group of developing founders were inspired and challenged by the municipal preprimary schools of Reggio Emilia, Italy. Those founders observed firsthand the sophisticated, articulate, intricate expression of ideas and feelings and theories produced by these very young children.

I wonder to what extent Donald Graves and other writing workshop pioneers were aware of what was happening in Reggio Emilia. On that same page of *Write from the Start*, there is a quote from Gregory Bateson's collection of essays *Mind and Nature*. Graves and Stuart quote Bateson's words: "Break the pattern that connects the items of learning, and you necessarily destroy all quality" (Bateson 2002, 7). When I picked up *Write from the Start* recently, I was startled to find that quote there, in those opening pages of the book that had inspired me to become a teacher. I knew the quote well but had forgotten it in that context. I've become familiar with Bateson's writings and that quote in particular because of how often it is referenced in the writings of philosophers and theorists from Reggio Emilia. In the context of Italian early childhood schools that were built as an anti-fascist effort out of the rubble of the Second World War, a commitment to the patterns and connections of learning had developed. In the context of early literacy in American schools, a commitment to these same patterns had led, at least in part, to an understanding of writing process and the development of writing workshop.

In the first chapter of *Write from the Start*, Graves and Stuart establish a case for writing workshop as a productive response

to an adult mindset that interferes with children's writing development. That mindset includes assumptions like these:

- Most adults think children can't write until they can read.

- Most adults think children can't write until they successfully complete spelling, punctuation, and grammar exercises.

- Most adults think children can't write without assignments, pictures, story starters, or even word lists to get them going.

- Most adults think children don't want to write. (Graves and Stuart 1985)

What if the ways in which writing is taught in early childhood classrooms have done more to perpetuate these beliefs than to disrupt them? What if traditional teaching practices create these assumptions, and the children's responses to them, and it's not the children themselves? Or their willingness to write? Or their ability to write? How might we create the conditions necessary for us to see something new, so we can rewrite the narrative we tell ourselves about children and writing? Or about play and learning? Or about the value of the arts?

Graves and Stuart wrote those statements about the beliefs of "most adults" over thirty years ago. To be clear, as I've worked directly with thousands of teachers over the last decade, it has not been my experience that most teachers have the same mindset as "most adults." As we've shared the stories of our experiences and research through workshops and publications, we've seen story workshop get picked up in places around the world, and we've celebrated as we've seen the delight and motivation of teachers who are seeing children write and play and share with a level of engagement and productivity they never thought possible. As children become more engaged, it seems, teachers do, too.

But beliefs about the limitations of children held by most adults set in motion expectations about what should happen in school that create tensions that are difficult to navigate for most teachers. Not only are the issues identified by Graves and Stuart still resonant in our culture and society, but we can add even more to the list:

🖋 Most adults think children (especially some children) have to choose between play and learning at school.

🖋 Most adults think that the arts in school are expendable and that story is nice but not necessary.

🖋 Most adults think that children's big emotions distract from the real work of the classroom.

🖋 Most adults think children (especially some children) won't pass standardized tests if their teachers don't stay on schedule with a scripted curriculum.

🖋 Most adults spend more energy worrying about where children are going next than they do attending to who they are right now.

🖋 Most adults don't give enough serious attention to the powerful reciprocity between childhood and adulthood.

Our classrooms reflect the way we look at things. If we want to develop classrooms that reflect what children can do, not only how well they can do what we ask them to do, we need a different approach. Additionally, we need resources that can help us stay grounded in what most teachers really know about children: they are curious and competent communicators who have stories to tell and who want to make connections to the stories other people tell so they can find their place in the human family.

> "The children of the future need stories to wonder and learn so that they can be curious. If you're curious, you don't make stereotypes and when you don't make stereotypes, you don't discriminate against other people. Which is good. Because discrimination doesn't make us a happy community."
>
> —Chloe (age 11)

Donald Graves writes,

> Children want to write. They want to write the first day they attend school. This is no accident. Before they went to school they marked up walls, pavements, newspapers with crayons, chalk, pens or pencils . . . anything that makes a mark. The child's mark says, "I am."
>
> "No you aren't," say most school approaches to the teaching of writing. We ignore the child's urge to show what he knows. We underestimate the urge because of a lack of understanding of the writing process and what children do in order to control it. Instead, we take the control away from children and place unnecessary road blocks in the way of their intentions. Then we say, "They don't want to write. How can we motivate them?" (Graves 2003, 3)

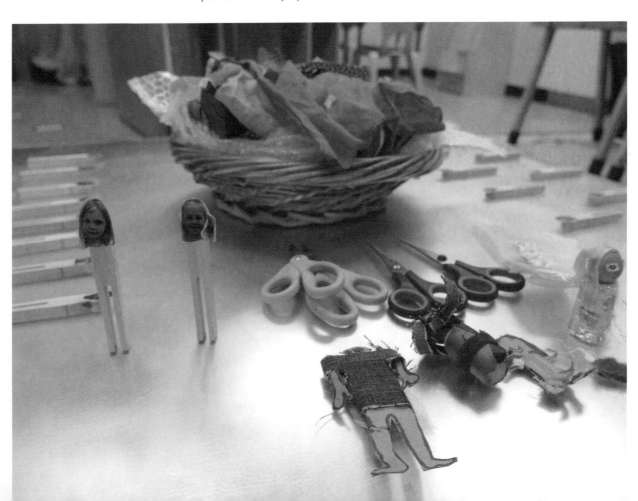

Graves seems to be arguing the same points that Malaguzzi crafted into his famous poem "The Hundred Languages of Children." I encourage you to pause right now and find the poem online if it is not familiar to you. Take a moment to read it and reflect on the similarity of concern between Malaguzzi and Graves.

Both authors declare that the child arrives at school already having exercised efforts to make marks on the world—to say, "I am." The child already knows hundreds of ways to make those marks. The child is learning to talk so he can make his mark through story, in order to make sense of experience and to express it and to find connection and belonging in his own community, wherever he may be.

Things like heads and hearts, reason and dream, or science and imagination are not things that come apart easily for children. It hurts. And what is tragic for us all is the fact that, as hard as they are to take apart, they are even more difficult to get back together again. Break the pattern and destroy the quality.

In Reggio Emilia, as the Second World War ended, and the town had been reduced to rubble, citizens of the community asked, "What can we do to ensure

> **"You can't play without thinking."**
>
> —Eli (age 9)

this never happens again?" and "How can we grow a citizenry that will be less likely to destroy itself in the future?" Loris Malaguzzi reflected on this time of hope and imagination and repair in the community by saying, "History can be changed, and is changed by taking possession of it, starting with the destiny of the children" (in Barazzoni 2000, 15). This is the work of teachers. When we are willing to invite the biggest questions we can possibly ask into our classrooms, we can take possession of history by working in solidarity with the destiny of the children.

When we are trying to come up with solutions to big problems, the questions we ask matter. They create the context in which we make decisions. When we aren't explicitly curious about questions that look beyond skills and compliance, our choices still create a response to those questions. When we relinquish possession of history—when we don't actively consider the kind of world we are trying to create as we do the work we do—we still make the world. Will it be the one we were hoping for? Teachers who work with young children are in the privileged position of supporting the habits and dispositions and attitudes of the citizenry that will create that world.

> **Reflection:** *Asking the Right Questions*
>
>
>
> What are the biggest questions you are asking as you consider your work with children? What patterns exist between these questions, the work you do with children, and the world you want to see?
>
> If you want to do more, I highly recommend using the resources available from the Right Question Institute (https://rightquestion.org/) to organize the development of your big questions with colleagues.

What Can You Expect from This Book?

There are five elements that make up the structure of story workshop: preparation, provocation, invitation and negotiation, story creation, and story sharing. This book is organized around that structure.

In **CHAPTER 1** we'll consider the case for story workshop. What does the research tell us about the importance of play, the arts, and story to the

Video I.1 Kerry, Aeriale, Rosemary, and Melissa in Conversation.

See page ix on how to access this video.

healthy development of human beings? How does that research inform story workshop practice?

CHAPTER 2 will begin a journey through the structure of story workshop. Preparation is the first element, taking place each day prior to the children's arrival. It includes organizing the space, time, and teacher-research tools to support productive encounters with and between the children.

CHAPTER 3 addresses provocation. We define the daily routine that launches story workshop as a time for teachers to bring a question to children to engage and support their interests and curiosity.

In **CHAPTER 4** we'll explore the element of invitation and negotiation. Here, teachers make agreements with children about how they will spend their time.

CHAPTER 5 focuses on story creation. This is time each day in which children look for, find, invent, and write stories. Children play with materials, talk to each other, and tell and write their stories.

In **CHAPTER 6** the journey leads us to story sharing. Teachers want the work of one creation time to influence the next and for the ideas of children to inspire others in this community of inquirers and authors.

CHAPTER 7 serves as a conclusion to our exploration of the story workshop terrain.

Each chapter includes several features:

🖋 **Pictures of Practice:** These snapshots give you windows into stories of story workshop in classrooms serving children between the ages of three and eight. This documentation describes the moves of the teachers as they work alongside the children but puts the focus on the work the children are capable of doing when these conditions created by story workshop are present.

🖋 **Writing Workshop Connections:** These sections articulate the relationship of each element to its writing workshop cousin. We provide this feature to support teachers who are familiar with writing workshop to find connections and to invite relationship.

🖋 **Try This:** This feature offers teachers new to story workshop ideas for dipping their toes in the practice. Perhaps you'll begin by considering the role of materials and play during your literacy structures. Perhaps you'll reflect more on the ways in which you document the work of the children and use it to plan for instruction. Or perhaps you'll encourage the children to share their work with one another in new ways. There is no need to try everything at once and no need to follow any strict sequence. There are many ways to start your own journey into story workshop—many small steps you can take, each of which, as long as you are willing to be curious yourself and keep asking big questions, will give you a little more courage to try something more.

🖋 **Materials Explorations and Reflection Questions:** These sections invite readers to engage with materials and questions. We have found that adults respond in similar ways as children do when they get their hands on materials, and these experiences promote an empathy for the perspective of children. I'll guide you through experiences you can do on your own or in study groups with colleagues. Each chapter includes multiple invitations to reflect on your own practices and to clarify your beliefs, values, hopes, and intentions as an educator.

🖋 **Action Steps:** At the end of each chapter, these steps offer you quick access to tangible suggestions for getting started or support for what to do next.

🖋 **Educator Interviews:** Between chapters, you'll be introduced to educators who have embraced story workshop in settings outside of Opal School. These pieces are excerpts from transcripts of conversations between Kerry Salazar and each educator. We hope you'll enjoy the bonus online video (Video I.1), where you will get a chance to watch Kerry and three of these teachers talk with each other about their approaches. (See the Online Resources for this and other videos.)

"Stories are maps of your life."

—Kellen (age 4)

CHAPTER ONE
The Case for Story Workshop

What Is Story Workshop?

Story workshop is a structure and approach that supports language and literacy development in the preschool and primary grades. Adults work alongside children as they explore prepared environments and experiences and share stories. Together they wonder:

- Where do stories live?

- What stories do I want the world to hear?

- What stories do I need to tell?

- How do stories influence me and our community?

- How do my stories become part of my community, and how do the stories of others in my community become a part of me?

At Opal School, story workshop takes place four or five days a week and lasts up to ninety minutes. Teachers in other schools, some of whom you'll meet in pages between chapters, have developed their own rhythms of story workshop that work for them in their unique settings. In every story workshop, adults invite children to imagine, write, edit, revise, publish, and share their stories. Prepared spaces and organized materials inspire and entice children to overflow with thoughts and ideas and memories and imagination. Materials like blocks, paint, water, sand, colored pencils, and loose-parts collage become the vehicles for the children's stories and act as inspiration as they capture them on paper as increasingly skilled writers. Adults facilitate children to engage as a thought community, listening to one another's stories and considering their influence on their lives and in their classroom. They construct meaning together as they make sense of the world they experience together.

There are five elements that make up the structure of story workshop, which form the organizing principle for this book:

1. *Preparation* happens prior to the children's arrival. It includes organizing materials and environments specifically designed to support both the children's story creation and the teacher's research.

2. *Provocation* is the whole-group session that begins each story workshop. It includes a proposal the teacher introduces to the children to engage, sustain, and extend their interests and curiosity.

3. *Invitation and negotiation* is the transition between provocation and creation. It is intended to support each child with a plan to get started.

4. *Story creation* makes up the bulk of a session of story workshop. It is a time for using the arts and play as well as writing to make meaning, to imagine, to create, and to share stories.

5. *Story sharing* brings closure to story workshop each day. It is a time for building community through story and reflection.

The organizational structure is sequential, but I encourage you to dive in anywhere that you feel most comfortable. The element of the structure you are most curious about and in which you can find the most connections to your current work would be a good place to take beginning steps into the theory and practice of story workshop. Give yourself time, and observe your students, who will have plenty to teach you!

Humans Are Storytellers

Stories—the ability to create them, the ability to learn from them, the ability to teach with them—are uniquely human. In a book about story making, it seems important to spend some time up front thinking about how this came to be. It also seems important to spend some time thinking about how it *comes* to be, fresh in each newly human being. First our bodies feel things and we need to make sense of the connections between our bodies and the world. To make sense of these perceptual encounters with the world in its myriad forms, we make use of the strategy unique to our species: story. We reach toward others like us. Because we are human, we learn language. And as our capacity for language grows, we continue to learn, in one way or another, how to better tell our stories.

Long before we have words, we read the world. And though our ability to say what we mean is limited, our capacity to explore and create is boundless. Sensory perception results in physiological responses, and we need to make sense of them. We feel, but we don't know what the feelings mean, and we don't know the extent

> The mind assembles experiences and constructs stories from them. It never pauses. It evolves continuously. As old stories fade with time, new ones are laid upon them. At the highest level of creativity, all human beings talk and sing and they tell stories.
>
> —Edward O. Wilson, *The Origins of Creativity* (2018, 27)

to which those feelings define who we are. We don't yet know how those feelings bind us to others. The people around us, who are associated with virtually all of our experiences as we try to make sense of things, are using words, and because our survival depends on our belonging to these people, we soon decipher those words and start to borrow them. Over time we become increasingly interested in what others have to share—in other people's stories—because hearing from them helps us know better who we are, where we are, what's happening, and what might happen next. We learn that, by sharing our stories, we have the power to put ideas and memories and emotions into other people's brains. Through story, we ensure that we're not alone.

The Biology of Story

In *The Origins of Creativity*, Edward Wilson explains story from an evolutionary, biological perspective:

> **It was evidently in *Homo habilis*, present in Africa between 2.3 and 1.5 million years ago, that the swerve began that ended in modern humanity. In its segment of prehistory, the cranial capacity, hence brain size, rose from 500 to 800 cc, well above the size of the modern chimpanzee. It grew again, to that of *Homo erectus* (about 1,000 cc) and thence to *Homo sapiens* (averaging 1,300 cc or more). The momentous threshold was crossed by the early *Homo sapiens*: the larger brain provided larger memory, leading to the construction of internal storytelling, then for the first time in the history of life to true language. From language came our unprecedented creativity and culture. (2018, 105)**

Our brains evolved to tell stories and those stories built the world that continues to evolve through story. Wilson continues, "Whales grow to great size by seining tiny crustaceans, bats fly at night by echolocation, birds fly at night by the polar magnetic field. Humans think" (2018, 86). Story is a fundamental and unique kind of thinking that humans do.

We are not a species well designed to thrive sitting at separate desks or walking single file, or limited to video conferencing. We need contact in order to survive. A hundred thousand years ago, our ancestors were social creatures who divided roles and relied on cooperation. Use of increasingly sophisticated language evolved because it resulted in higher survival and reproductive rates. "By any measures of liberation and empowerment, language is not just a creation of humanity, it *is* humanity" (Wilson 2018, 26). First we have experiences. We think about them, and *then* we develop language to tell our thoughts using a variety of abstract symbol systems, including words. Humanity relies on this unique ability not only for survival but as a condition for imagination, freedom, identity, and belonging. And, as it turns out, imagination, freedom, identity, and belonging *are* survival because we make the world, and the quality of the world we make relies on the strength of those capacities.

In an essay for *Harper's Magazine*, Ferris Jabr describes our relationship to story this way:

> **We give life to the stories we tell, imagining entire worlds and preserving them on rock, paper, and silicon. Stories sustain us: they open paths of clarity in the chaos of existence, maintain a record of human thought, and grant us the power to shape our perceptions of reality. The coevolution of humans and stories may not be one of the oldest partnerships in the history of life on Earth, but it is certainly one of the most robust. As a psychic creature simultaneously parasitizing and nourishing the human mind, narrative was so thoroughly successful that it is now all but inextricable from language and thought. Stories live through us, and we live through stories. (2019)**

Children seek tools to tell the stories that are living through them in order to make sense of what it means to be alive.

The Brain Behind the Stories

We are each born with a brain prepared to investigate and make sense of the world in partnership with our body. We arrive preloaded with all the neurons we'll ever have, and they fire constantly, seeking and making connections, ensuring that we're learning all the time. By the age of six, our brains have grown to 90 percent of their adult size, and the space between those neurons we've had from the beginning are buzzing with pathways that have become established as the basic architecture of the brain we'll use forever. Those pathways are developed in direct relationship to the experiences we have and the environments we grow up in (Center on the Developing Child 2019). Neuroscientist Lisa Barrett (2017a) said, "The neuroscience is crystal clear: brains wire themselves to their surroundings. A developing infant brain requires wiring instructions from the world around it. Without proper nourishment, both nutritional and social, that little brain will not develop to its fullest."

As we use the neural pathways created by these wires, they get stronger—for better or for worse. Brains use these pathways to make ongoing predictions about what will happen next in order to decide what to do next. This is one of the brain's most basic, primal functions (Barrett 2017b). Emotions themselves are a kind of guess your brain makes based on what has happened in the past. In *Emotions, Learning, and the Brain*, Mary Immordino-Yang puts it this way: "[Emotions] pertain to what we think we know about the world at the current time, interpreted in light of our past experiences and our imagined possible futures, using our available skills. . . . They rely on subjective, cognitive interpretations of situations and their accompanying embodied reactions" (2016, 19). Our brains look forward, in search of connections to what's behind, continually seeking patterns. The brain asks, "What about this experience is most like my past experience?" Reading situations through that lens, we make our predictions, assumptions, and decisions, and the wires get stronger. Old stories seek ways to continue that make the world make sense. Through story, we organize our perceptions.

What Does It Mean to Make Meaning?

Literacy researcher Brian Cambourne spent years dedicated to bridging the gaps we struggle to cross between learning, meaning, and biology. His research led to an understanding that human beings create meaning in order to make sense of the world, and that making sense of the world is the only way we survive. Unlike any other species, evolution ensured that humans make meaning from a variety of abstract symbol systems, including words. Because this ability is a species survival trait, evolution also ensured that its acquisition is as "fail-safe" as possible (Cambourne 2015b). Cambourne (2015a) writes, "Rather than subconsciously thinking about learning and knowledge as some kind of 'stuff' which exists in the world and which the learner somehow had to 'acquire,' I began thinking about learning and knowledge as something which was constructed by a learner using symbols." Meaning comes from within the child as they make sense of things through perception, prediction, and connection, becoming themselves.

Children have a right to high-quality, vigorous instruction intended to support their academic skills within the discipline of literacy. But those skills must be inextricably linked to stories—to the paths every child determines need clarity in their own life. Increasing literacy skill should be seen as a means by which the stories flowing through each of us are supported as the effort they are to make better sense of the world in which we experience the complexity of our everyday lives. Literacy skills are no end in and of themselves, and treating them as such takes us further from the capacity every child has to use them to find and share our stories.

Adults can influence children's stories but can't write them. What we *can* do is create conditions that invite and encourage children to make meaning of

things we agree are meaningful. We can create conditions that invite children to construct learning and knowledge in an environment that offers access to a wide range of materials available to help them express their thoughts, ideas, and feelings through a range of abstract symbols. We can put the power of shaping perception, making predictions, and seeking connections squarely where it resides—in the child. And we can use the opportunity to understand what they are understanding so we can better influence, invite, and inspire them to move forward. This is what story workshop is for.

Stories in School

School should be prepared for stories because stories don't wait for school. School should be designed with the understanding that it is its own kind of made-up story we've learned to believe in and can therefore change. From the brain's perspective, school is just another perceptual experience, indistinguishable from "real" life (Caine and Caine 1997). It is a space, like all others, that creates an embodied reaction that both is caused by and informs what we think we already know and what we can imagine will happen next. If making meaning with and through stories is integral to humanity, stories are already integral to school.

This is not so much a book about why we tell children stories, or how to write stories, or even how to read them. It is not a book that intends to persuade the reader of the many good reasons that humans are so hungry to consume stories and why they are of such high nutritional value. Though we

are, and they are. And though it isn't entirely possible to talk about stories without talking about why we consume them, this book focuses more on *why we must invite children to tell their own*—about how we learn to live in the world we make through stories and why it is such a deep biological need for children to create them.

No matter who they are or where they come from, no matter how many words they know, children arrive in school telling stories. They have prior knowledge based on experience that leads them to make predictions including and informed by emotion. Because they are meaning makers, they seek and construct meaning. Pages 10–11 offer an example of what that might sound like and look like with a very young child.

"I want to hear your connections!"
—Simon (age 5)

Where Stories Live

Story workshop is designed to create conditions for children to think about and make stories from the world they have experienced—the things they wonder, notice, and imagine and the things that concern them. It is designed to embrace the interdependent, ecological system of experience, perception, cognition, imagination, community, and identity. We find stories in the forest we're walking through, the lump of clay that takes shape within our hands, the expression on a friend's face, the blocks; we find them by looking closely at an object and capturing what we see, working collaboratively on developing a story through paper lines and paint, and exploring a collection of interesting loose parts. We want to know if others see things the way we do.

Pictures of Practice
Stella's Story

Stella was a three-year-old child who experienced a language delay and had been talking for only a few months when she wanted to tell a story about her family to her teacher, Caroline. She said, "A flu shot hurts. My mommy got a flu shot. Then my Max got a flu shot on my mommy's lap. And I got a flu shot. And my Sophie got a flu shot, too. And my Sophie got a flu shot, too. And, the end." Caroline assumed she was finished, but then Stella kept going, and Caroline nodded, continuing to write. Stella said, "Then we goed. Then we goed to home. Then we goed to school."

Caroline said, "Can I read it back to you?" Stella shook her head. So Caroline confirmed, "No?"

"Are you sure?" Caroline then teased. Stella laughed. Caroline continued, "Are you sure I got all your words down? Are you sure you don't want to hear it to make sure?"

Stella took a peek at what Caroline had been doing on the clipboard with her pen. And this time, Stella said, "Yeah. I want to hear it."

Video 1.1 Stella Tells a Story

See page ix on how to access this video.

Caroline began to read. Stella's facial expressions give us a window into the experience she had as her own words came back to her through Caroline.

Stella had a strong emotional response to hearing Caroline read her story back to her. This experience and these emotions demonstrate the power of the opportunity to share stories to find out what we mean and to realize that our stories can live in other people, that we can see ourselves in others, and that we're not alone. Immordino-Yang writes, "When educators fail to appreciate the importance of students' emotions, they fail to appreciate a critical force in students' learning. One could argue, in fact, that they fail to appreciate the very reason that students learn at all" (2016, 40). We can be confident that as this emotional experience wired together in Stella's brain, along with this literacy experience, she moved forward engaged and wanting more.

We can design our classrooms to offer all children rich, provocative materials that produce images through play. Images support children not only to express what they cannot yet say in words alone but also to see what they have to say in ways they cannot without the images the materials help them create. All children have a right to learning environments in school where they are invited to use symbols to construct meaning so they can make sense of their world and share with others. Because, invited or not, as human beings, this is what they're doing, whether we're listening or not. Everyone benefits when the classroom is designed for this process to be joyful.

It is an unfortunate truth that in many classrooms, with best intentions, skills are valued over stories. When this is the case, in a well-intentioned effort to instruct, we don't see the child, but the child learns to see themselves as we do. In her book *Culturally Responsive Teaching and the Brain: Promoting Authentic Engagement and Rigor Among Culturally and Linguistically Diverse Students*, Zaretta Hammond defines the deficit thinking paradigm that perpetuates injustices and inequities in our society and culture, including curriculum that places skill over story:

> When operating from a deficit thinking paradigm, educators and policymakers believe that culturally and linguistically diverse students fail in school because of their own deficiencies. . . . This deficit perspective suggests that efforts to improve academic achievement should be focused on "fixing" students . . . rather than shifting the school culture to support intellective capacity building and identity-safe classrooms so that students can access their academic potential. As a result, teachers' deficit-oriented attributions of student performance influence their instructional decision making, resulting in giving students less opportunity for engaging curricula, interesting tasks, and culturally congruent ways of learning. (2015, 59)

When we structure opportunities for children to use a diverse range of symbol systems to create meaning, to revisit, to manipulate, to extend, to refine, to build on, to share, and to communicate with others as a first priority and every day at school, our classrooms become the places where we can repair injustice. They become places where we build common ground and explore a healthy and productive relationship with difference. Doing this work supports us to become more comfortable with uncertainty and diverse perspectives. As we strengthen our own capacity to observe and listen to the stories children share, our classrooms become places where we can all learn to be more curious and less afraid of taking risks and of things that feel uncertain.

In an article titled "Toward Greater Equity in Literacy Education: Story-making and Non-Mainstream Students," Nina Mikkelsen offers a challenge:

> **So how do we define a non-mainstream child really? Have we come even close to understanding this elusive term? Or have we been simply—and conveniently—classifying students in order to design new teaching strategies, without fundamentally changing ourselves or our feelings about people? Today we need to find ways of transforming classrooms that involve what children *do* in these classrooms, but not before we consider how we really feel about these children and what they *are* outside the classrooms. If we really want to enable all children to participate as equal and responsible members of the classroom culture (or the culture at large), no matter what the "stream," we must first find ways to transform ourselves. We must move from the notion of "I taught these children and they became more like me," to "I listened to children, and they grew more as themselves." (1990, 565)**

Story workshop gives us a path away from a damaging, deficit paradigm by structuring classroom practice that is responsive to and supportive of the behaviors that are our biological and evolutionary birthright as human beings. It creates conditions for us to listen to children in order to support them to grow as themselves—as citizen world-makers with imagination, agency, self-efficacy, and empathy who know they are in charge of their own story.

Resilience Relies on Imagination

The stories we tell about our experiences have power over our subsequent experiences. Our brains use what we've experienced to predict what we'll experience next and what emotions we'll have next, too. Resilience is a highly valuable habit of mind, but its strength relies on imagination. Our capacity for resilience is reliant on our capacity for story. When we need to find our way beyond the challenges of our lives, we need to be able to imagine the path, but we also need to have an ability to fluently piece together something we may not have yet considered using parts we haven't yet connected. That ability grows and strengthens through a practice of dialogue, which is, at its most essential, an encounter in the world that sets as its intention to transform the world (Freire 1997).

This kind of dialogue happened in a very profound way not so many years ago when a child arrived, quiet and shy, new to kindergarten. The class was involved in a long-term investigation of self. Through weeks of this investigation, this child had contributed very little of their own voice. On the day the teachers invited the children to share theories about how a body takes care of itself, however, this child was inspired to dialogue with the materials. In these materials the child found an opportunity to share their theory of anger and hurt—something their teachers sensed they had much experience with but had, as yet, been unable to support them to express. As the child began playing with the materials in the block area, with a hint of urgency in their voice, this child began to explain their theory of how anger is transformed in the body. With blocks in hand, the child was able to imagine the ways in which anger and sadness move through the body on their way to happiness again. While the child's hands moved and built with stones and blocks, the child told a story. The pieces and parts the student played with inspired the pieces and parts of a narrative to take form as a story the child could use to help themselves through future challenges.

Opportunity and time to play with materials in response to a provocative question invited this child to use story to influence the predictions the child's brain would make in the future. Immordino-Yang explains, "Emotions, like cognition, develop with maturity and experience. In this sense, emotions are skills—organized patterns of thoughts and behaviors that we actively construct in the moment and across our life spans to adaptively accommodate to various kinds of circumstances, including academic demands" (2016, 20). Creating conditions in which children have the opportunity to organize experience in ways that give them control over things that are hard, confusing, or traumatic creates practice with the skill of emotion, allowing children to learn that because they can be in charge of how they think about things, they can also be in charge of how they feel. In *Pedagogy of the Oppressed*, Paulo Freire writes, "If it is in speaking their word that people, by naming the world, transform it, dialogue imposes itself as the way by which they achieve significance as human beings" (1997, 69). Authentic dialogue (even if that dialogue is with materials) contributes to the development of agency and self-efficacy. In play, a person is in charge of their own story, allowing them to be adaptive in future possible circumstances because they know they can imagine a way forward. *They know they can.*

Emotions Are Skills We Practice in Story

We can learn to influence our own brain wiring by learning to pay attention to the stories we create and the emotions we feel, by sharing them with others, and by learning to listen and connect to the stories other people tell. Story workshop is designed to support this practice during the most critical years in which the brain is growing and building those pathways. Story workshop gives children practice being in charge of their own stories. It gives children practice with understanding that experiences aren't fixed and so neither are emotions. It helps them learn how to choose the way they want to feel about things. It invites them to create a vision for themselves and the way they want to live in the world—and it gives them permission to make the world they want to live in. It helps them learn the words to articulate not only their experience but also their emotions and all they imagine. Through words, they reach out and find connection with others. They perceive a response that creates emotion . . . and on it goes. This is the practice that promotes imagination, freedom, identity, and belonging.

In the following story, Caroline explores this interconnected web alongside a group of kindergarten children.

Pictures of Practice
Playing with Perspective

Any group of five-year-old children is composed of individuals who are as infused with emotion as all human beings are, all the time. They do not yet know the extent to which others experience emotion, or how differently they might experience emotion, or how emotion influences behavior. They feel. And, based on prior experience, they predict and they act. In any group, this combination of feeling, predicting, and acting creates misfires that, if not understood and repaired, will lead to ongoing problems. Caroline knew that exploring experiences connected to emotion would improve communication and nurture empathy and compassion. So she set up an experience with materials in story workshop that would invite dialogue.

Caroline chose tempera paint as the material that the children would use to explore and express their ideas, because it was a material that the children had experience with already, so they knew its properties well. Having done a lot of experimenting already with the material meant that they could be ready to *think with it*. (More on learning to think with materials in Chapter 2.)

In this case, Caroline also considered that the endless variety of colors tempera paint could become might prove to be an important attribute that would invite metaphorical thinking. The many shades and tints that could be created in tempera seemed like a potential point of connection with the many shades of emotion we all experience. Caroline predicted that this attribute would promote an abundance of language as children found their way into the stories of experience they'd had as they'd felt those nuanced shades.

Finally, Caroline was intentional about asking the children to make marks and lines because she wanted them to avoid symbols typically used to express an emotion, such as a smiley face for happy. She thought the children would find it an intriguing challenge to reflect on their emotions and communicate their understanding of their emotions through color and line.

I'll share a few of the children's images and the words they used to express their thinking about the meaning of emotion vocabulary after they had painted.

Caroline asked them, "Can you use colors and lines to capture the feeling of angry?"

One child explained, "I used brown and black and I made scribbles because angry things feel like scribbles. You might explode." (See Figure 1.1.)

Another said, "When I'm angry, it is a loud angry, like thunder and lightning." (See Figure 1.2.)

When Caroline looked at another child's color choices and design (see Figure 1.3), she was surprised. She was genuinely interested to know the child's thinking, because they weren't the colors Caroline predicted the children would select to interpret *angry*. She said, "Wow! Tell me about the lines and colors that you chose."

The child said, "The pinkness is I'm mad because my cheeks get pink. The redness comes out of my ears like fire coming out of your ears."

Caroline asked the children to represent the emotion of sad. The painting in Figure 1.4 came from a child who was experiencing a lot of upheaval at the time. Up to this point, she hadn't shared many stories or connections with the group, but with these materials in hand, and these particular invitations to consider emotion, she was deeply engaged and focused. These images helped everyone

Figure 1.1

Figure 1.2

Figure 1.3

Figure 1.4

Figure 1.5

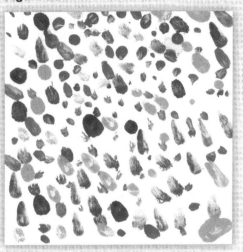

better understand the child's mental image of sadness. She explained, "The blue and black are my tears, the gray is my inside, and the red is my inside coming out as crying."

The example in Figure 1.5 helps us see how naturally human beings put story to work to make sense of experience. This child, who was new to the concept of story when she began school, said, "This little purple dot [lowest left] is the little boy in the woods. These are all the footprints going in all directions. He can't figure out which ones go to his mom and he is very sad."

These open-ended materials, and instructions to use the color and the lines they could make to express emotion, allowed the children to step inside the world of those emotions in a way that revealed deeply personal meaning. Use of the arts produced the language of story, which uncovered differences that encouraged curiosity and relationship within the community.

Very early on during this project, Caroline asked the children to select colors that represented happiness to them. Paul quickly picked up several containers, one of which was filled with black paint. Another child noticed this and said, "I don't think that black is a happy color."

Caroline asked her, "Why? What does black make you think of?"

The child looked up with a very sad expression and tears welling up in her eyes as she said quietly, "Sad. Black was the color that my mom wore to her brother's funeral, not so long ago."

Paul listened intently to what she said and then said, "Black makes me think of baseball. I love baseball!"

The use of the material itself allowed children glimpses into the stories of each other's lives and an opportunity to tangibly experience the complexity of perspective. Images produce words and words produce images. We can find this powerful reciprocity everywhere—in the paint, in the naming of emotions, and in each other.

Supporting Children to Grow as Themselves

Consider the ways in which Scouten (see the prelude), Stella, the child who found their story about anger in the blocks, and the children in the emotions project were working during story workshop, as Mikkelsen (1990) proposes, "as themselves." Take a moment to reflect on what was required of their teachers to position them to do so. How did the environment itself play a role?

Figures 1.6 and 1.7 capture what I think the physiological state referred to as relaxed alertness looks like in action. Closely related to the state of flow, as described by Mihaly Csikszentmihalyi (2008), relaxed alertness happens in an environment of low risk and high challenge. It is the optimal state of mind for learning, as opposed to another physiological state called downshifting, which happens when we feel a sense of disconnection, boredom, or helplessness. In a state of relaxed alertness, children can work as themselves—and teachers can, too. This kind of exercise of personal agency or self-efficacy is the opposite of downshifting (Caine and Caine 1997). Self-efficacy is a belief that one is in charge of one's own experience, and it is a prerequisite for agency. In the children's stories we've encountered so far in this book, it is possible to hear that self-efficacy, that voice that says, "I matter. I can."

Figures 1.6 and 1.7

In their book *Unleashing the Power of Perceptual Change: The Potential of Brain-Based Teaching*, Caine and Caine write:

> People downshift when they feel helpless. They . . . lose much of their capacity to think creatively and tolerate risk, uncertainty, and ambiguity. In effect, they experience the opposite of self-efficacy. By using power based almost exclusively on a command-and-control structure, educators induce helplessness and compliance . . . and reduce the willingness and ability of . . . students to take personal risks. Such risks are the hallmark of the exploration that accompanies genuine intellectual struggles. . . .
>
> When a teacher uses power to induce students to do what they are told, and when it is combined with lack of meaning and purpose and a passive "going along" with what students are asked to do, then such students are not in a low threat/high challenge mode, and genuine complex learning will not take place. . . .
>
> An education system that employs power and induces downshifting therefore prevents maximum learning. It restricts one's perspective, reflection, creative thinking, and ability to live with paradox and engage in most forms of higher-order thinking. . . .
>
> Throughout the system, the exercise of power over others and deference to power are prevalent and have a devastating effect. . . . The fear engendered also breeds a dependence on rules and bureaucracy and limits genuine learning and innovation. (1997, 95–97)

All of the young children that show up in early childhood classrooms all over the world arrive with growing brains, eager to connect with others, and each with the right to develop as themselves. Because adults control the environments and experiences children will have—because they constrain the boundaries of possibility children can explore—adults should ask themselves, always, about the influence of the conditions they create on the opportunity children have to turn capacity into ability. How can the limitations of adult imagination have the least impact on the limitless imagination of children? How do we break free of a deficit paradigm that keeps us all—children and adults—in a state of downshift?

Playing in School Develops Self-Efficacy

Play is the ultimate invitation into a state of relaxed alertness; high challenge and low risk are built right in. For young children, play is the optimal state for learning. This is not to say that in play, children don't experience downshifting. It happens all the time. (See Figure 1.8.) There is constant tension over who has the power to control the play. Play includes the opportunity to cycle through periods of downshifting and gives players practice with finding their way back to relaxed alertness.

Biologically speaking, we play because the world is an uncertain place and we use story to control the chaos. Self-efficacy gains strength from abundant opportunity to engage in play and tell stories, which produce and are produced by a sense of agency. As it takes our power away, downshifting represses play and reduces our opportunity to be in charge of our story. Downshifting often says, "You don't matter." It is an inevitable outcome of the deficit paradigm.

In the *New York Times*, the authors of the book *The Coddling of the American Mind* remind us of the importance of play:

> The most powerful person in the world is the storyteller.
>
> —Steve Jobs, in *Story Driven* (Jiwa 2018, 3)

Figure 1.8 "I am your friend!"

Mammals enter the world with unfinished nervous systems, and they require play—lots of it—to finish the job. The young human brain "expects" the child to engage in thousands of hours of play, including thousands of falls, scrapes, conflicts, insults, alliances, betrayals, status competitions, and even (within limits) acts of exclusion, in order to develop its full capacities.

But not all play is created equal. Peter Gray, a developmental psychologist at Boston College, studies the effects of "free play," which he defines as "activity that is freely chosen and directed by the participants and undertaken for its own sake, not consciously pursued to achieve ends that are distinct from the activity itself [2011, 444]." (Haidt and Lukianoff 2018)

While story workshop is not intended to meet Gray's definition of free play, it shares some of his most basic principles. In story workshop, teachers are committed to providing children with time and space to create stories that are "freely chosen and directed" by them. Story workshop is designed to help children reflect on their own play, learning to recognize that the things they do in play are the things that make us all human and that story is how we share in that humanity.

Story Making Is World Making

To cut to the chase, given that species survival is a critical concern on a dying planet, home to a population that is increasingly influenced by totalitarianism and experiencing the normalization of fascist thought, it is urgent that our schools, led by teachers and parents, figure out how to support strong self-efficacy, agency, and empathy—to create conditions that support compassionate citizen world-makers to grow as themselves. In *The Ecology of Imagination in Childhood*, Edith Cobb writes: "Worldmaking is learning in the widest sense, but it is also an adaptation to environment as nature, a search for higher levels of synthesis of self and world drawn from the recognition that outer and inner worlds are interdependent aspects of reality, rather than independent states" (1993, 66). World making is an encapsulation of our relationship with the world as an unending reciprocal exchange that is, at once, sensorial, embodied, emotional, social, artistic, and intellectual. The greater our awareness of our world-making powers, the greater are the chances that we will understand that what we do to the world, the world does to us.

With noted inspiration from Brené Brown's 2018 book, *Dare to Lead*, I invite you to take some time to consider the dispositions that nurture citizen world-makers that matter most to you.

Reflection: *Dispositions That Nurture Citizen World-Makers*

Read over the following list. What *three* words would you choose to encapsulate your *strongest* beliefs about what is most important when it comes to world-making? When I think about the skills and dispositions that lead citizen world-makers to thrive in today's world, I land on the following. Your list is likely different, so feel free to cross some out and add some in.

justice	inventiveness	humor
equity	innovation	reciprocity
voice	problem-solving	interdependence
agency	problem seeking	perspective taking
empathy	leadership	community
collaboration	engagement	reading
listening	vision	writing
power	trust	connection
empowered	play	flexibility
imagination	art	generosity
uncertainty	meaning making	hope
inquiry	emotional literacy	care
curiosity	compassion	self-efficacy
creativity	self-compassion	

Circle your three words. Write them down in a journal.

I recognize that limiting yourself to three might feel hard. But, as Brown writes, "if everything on the list is important, then nothing truly is a driver for you. It's just a gauzy list of feel-good words" (2018, 187. Our task is to move from gauze to drivers—because I don't believe that anyone reading this book would seriously disagree with anything on the list. But choosing a focus will help you grow the world that lives inside each word until it is vibrant and thriving in your practice. Take some time to reflect on how those three words come up for you as you think about the stories from the classroom I've shared so far. What questions do these words inspire you to ask as you consider those stories?

Asking Beautiful Questions to Guide Story Workshop

The questions we ask matter. They create the context in which we make the decisions that make the world. When we don't actively consider the kind of world we are trying to create as we do the work we do, we still make the world. Will it be the one we hope for?

In an interview with Krista Tippett, poet David Whyte spoke about shaping a beautiful mind as a discipline in itself. He went on to say:

> **A beautiful question shapes a beautiful mind. The ability to ask beautiful questions, often, in very unbeautiful moments, is one of the great disciplines of a human life. And a beautiful question starts to shape your identity as much by asking it as it does by having it answered. You don't have to do anything about it. You just have to keep asking, and before you know it, you will find yourself actually shaping a different life, meeting different people, finding conversations that are leading you in those directions that you wouldn't even have seen before. Also, one way I've come to think about questions, the power of questions, is that questions elicit answers in their likeness. You call forth something beautiful by asking a beautiful question. (Whyte 2019)**

I hope you are ready to ask lots of questions—raising the odds that at least some of them will be beautiful! I hope you are ready to play and delight and struggle and learn alongside and in the company of children. The most important role of the teacher in story workshop is to habitually ask questions, to think in questions—the kinds of questions that you do not already know the answer to; the kinds of questions worth living with; the kinds of questions that you are genuinely curious about. These are beautiful questions asked by people who are willing to grow their own sense of self-efficacy. They are beautiful because they invite an ongoing process of reflection. Or, as Elliot Eisner might say, they are beautiful because "they invite the most precious of human abilities to take wing. . . [speaking of] imagination, the neglected stepchild of American education" (Eisner 2006, 44).

The imagination of children relies on the imagination of the adult—and children can't practice self-efficacy if the adults around them don't practice it, too. In her book *The Faraway Nearby*, Rebecca Solnit writes, "We think we tell stories, but stories often tell us, tell us to love or to hate, to see or to be blind. Often, too often, stories saddle us, ride us, whip us onward, tell us what to do, and we do it without questioning. The task of learning to be free requires learning to hear them, to question them, to pause and hear silence, to name them, and then to become the storyteller" (2014, 4). If we do this together, before we know it, we'll have reclaimed our place as the storytellers.

Action Steps: Enrich Your Story Workshop Practice

This is a little book with a lot of information packed into a relatively small package. It is intended to be a resource that offers each reader an invitation to find their own starting place and a reason to keep coming back for more. At the end of each chapter, I offer a few suggestions for further exploration related to story workshop.

- If you are inspired by the idea of teacher research, immerse yourself in Karen Gallas' book *Imagination and Literacy* (2003). Let it help you strengthen your practice as a teacher-researcher. Write this quote of hers on the front page of a new journal: "Literacy is a process of merging who we are with what we show we can do" (100). Commit to reflecting on this elusive and complex idea at least once a month as you move through a school year and experiment with story workshop. Keep your reflections in your journal. Try reflecting with materials as well as writing.

- If you want to know more about how the way you think about something (the story you tell) influences the way you feel, make a commitment to develop a habit of reframing your experiences in the coming months. Learn to catch yourself telling a story about something that happened to you, something you think you believe, or an assumption about someone's intent. We do this constantly. Our brains love this efficiency. Reflect on what happens when you tell another story—that is, change the story, telling it a different way. Think to yourself: "What else could it be?" How do your emotions change?

If you want to create beautiful questions, make it a habit to ask them! What are the biggest questions you are asking as you consider your work with children? What patterns exist between these questions, the work you do with children, and the world you want to see? What other questions do these questions inspire?

EDUCATOR INTERVIEW: YOUR IDEAS MATTER

Excerpted from an interview with Melinda Hayward, preschool teacher
Prescott Elementary School, Parkrose School District, Oregon

PRESCOTT ELEMENTARY SCHOOL is a 100 percent free and reduced-lunch school, which means that 100 percent of our families experience poverty. Our preschool operates a needs-based enrollment system. The families, which have no other options for preschool, speak more than fourteen different languages.

I see story workshop as an equity piece and a culturally responsive practice—looking at it as support for our students who are super diverse, who speak zero English. They come in from all sorts of different cultures, and I see it as this opportunity to give them space to get the message, "Your ideas are important, your ideas matter, and you don't have to read in English or write in English to be

You can design provocations to promote sensory experience.

able to share them and for them to have value here." Of course all of the literacy learning is embedded into our big thinking, but I think it's the social-emotional growth within each child, of recognizing "I have ideas, my friends have ideas, and sometimes my friends' ideas inspire my ideas. What I have to say is important. And what my friends have to say is important" that is so valuable.

This year everything in our classroom that has a sensory component is high-interest for our group, possibly because a lot of them have experienced trauma. Having a sensory component lowers anxiety and helps them get grounded into the work. I've found I need to have a variety of spaces. I need to have spaces where one person can work alone if that's what they're feeling like they need. I also need a space where partners can go, or a space where there can be big, louder activities, like the big block area or the dramatic play [space].

Trying to find little nooks and crannies lowers the stress and anxiety of the group, because they always know there is space for them in a place where they feel safe and cared for. When we start the year, there is often a sort of feeling of scarcity, and tension, and then slowly the children relax into the flexibility and learn patience, [and they are] able to say, "It's going to be there for me when I need it, and if it's not there I can ask for it, and if I have a plan my teacher is going to be OK with it." They start to trust a little bit more. It's a relational environment.

As a new group is figuring out how to manage their choices, and I'm observing them, I try to think of every action as giving us more information. So if a child is dumping loose parts everywhere (and this has happened), I think they are probably craving more sensory opportunities in the room. That's something I can do to support them; it's a change I can make in the environment, instead of demanding the child to change.

This year, there's a child named Wes in our group who has a passion for dinosaurs and animals. He had been working with little chick characters and other loose parts, and he created a story about "Chickasaurus." I took a photo of his work and when it was sharing time, I projected the image. Wes has a speech ISSP [individual support services plan] and is a little bit hesitant to talk in front of groups, but he got up and shared the whole Chickasaurus story in front of everyone. They were amazed at all the details he had for animals and habitats, and you could see so much pride in Wes as he was able to call on friends that had questions and wonderings and find out what else they noticed about his story.

I have to come back to the equity piece. I've noticed with anyone—it doesn't matter if they're older or younger, or an English speaker or a non-English speaker, or they are nonverbal and they have an ISSP, or experience disabilities of other kinds—story workshop offers a way that everyone can share their love of stories together. It builds a stronger community. It allows us to see that we all have agency—we all have ideas that matter, and we find out that sharing them is fun, exciting, and so important. These are experiences that everyone has a right to.

Dear Kimie, I love you. But I have a feeling you are called a teacher and you don't just like . . . you know . . . teach us things. You do everything with us, all kinds of things, and we have meetings and reflections and we learn things. But why are you called a teacher when you don't teach us things in classes like a baking class or a math class? You ask us lots of questions and we do lots of things all the time. Is that being a teacher, too, Kimie?

—Love, Eli (age 3)

CHAPTER TWO
Preparation

P reparation is the organization of the classroom environment and experience specifically to support both the children's story creation and the teacher's research. In Videos 2.1 and 2.2, you'll see teachers preparing for story workshop. In Video 2.1, teachers discuss the ways they make decisions about materials and experiences. In Video 2.2, you're invited on a tour of a classroom organized to support story creation.

Video 2.1 Preparing the Environment for Stories

See page ix on how to access this video.

What Is Preparation?

A teacher practices two kinds of preparation before children arrive for story workshop. This chapter focuses on both: (1) the preparation teachers do to get themselves ready to listen to children, meet them where they are, and learn alongside them and (2) the preparation they do as they organize a physical environment that supports research, relationship,

Video 2.2 Touring a Classroom Prepared for Stories with Lauren Adams

Tour and talk with teachers as they prepare for story workshop. See page ix on how to access this video.

and the construction of meaningful language and literacy. In this chapter, we'll make connections between the preparation teachers do for themselves and the preparation they do for the children as we break each category into two parts: *setting intentions* and *documenting* (teachers) and *environment* and *materials* (physical space).

Images throughout this chapter are snapshots of classroom environments prepared to inspire, sustain, and extend the stories of the children who work and play there in story workshop.

As you play, what stories will you discover in these materials?

What happens as these color friends play together? Does a story wake up for you?

How will you use wire and fabric to research why stories are important?

Writing Workshop Connection: Preparation

When it is your goal to support a productive, rich, and lively writing workshop, materials matter. Children benefit when there are selections of interesting paper to choose from, journals to use, good writing materials, staplers, tape, and other interesting office supplies. Some teachers prepare a set of blank books made of stapled paper. There might be clipboards to make it easier for children to write where they are most comfortable. There are tools to support the use of the alphabet and maybe a personal dictionary of some kind. Maybe there are folders that help children organize their work and keep track of goals they've developed through conferences of various kinds. Writing workshop teachers also have tools for their own organization. They keep track of things. They take notes about their observations. They carefully plan minilessons and genre studies to support the children to work from their strengths and to engage deeply and skillfully with the process of writing. All of these things are true when it comes to story workshop as well. Each of the next four chapters includes an explicit connection to writing workshop. The intention of this feature is to support a relationship between the two structures and provide a familiar jumping-off point into what is distinctive about story workshop.

A writing
center prepared
for children
ages 3–5

Preparing Ourselves for Stories:
We Are All Protagonists

In the musical version of Roald Dahl's *Matilda* (Minchin 2013), the protagonist and title character wonders in song whether others see red in their minds the same way she does in hers. If there really is no way of knowing that red will mean the same thing in your head and mine, the implications for parenting, for diplomacy, for governing, and for teaching—the work that many would say depends most on being able to deliver information, skills, concepts, and knowledge from one head to another—are considerable. Being curious about this complexity (and trying not to be overwhelmed by it) is important to the preparation of a structure that will support children to tell their stories and teachers to listen to them, without presuming they see things the same way. Preparation for story workshop is a process of preparing to acknowledge the child in the role of protagonist of their own story. It isn't always convenient to take that perspective—the one in which you realize that the story you are telling, the one in which *you* are the protagonist, does not match the one anyone else is telling.

It helps to imagine this dilemma from the perspective of a parent, where the relationship between adult and child is, arguably, most dramatic. A child arrives in the midst of a parent's life story already in progress and plays a huge part in that story. Slowly, and sometimes painfully, the parent begins to realize that there is another story being told—the one that belongs to the child.

When my own three children reached an age where they could offer critiques of the story I was telling of my life with them in it, I was shocked, like most parents, into a vital recognition that their stories weren't mine. They

were a part of mine, but they weren't mine. I remember wondering: "If this is true, what are the implications for our experience together? What if I'm telling the story wrong?" All these years, I've been sharing an environment with my children, engaging with them, loving them more than I imagined possible—and they have been there with me. But they have been making their own meanings all along. And those meanings have been different from mine. As a vital part of their world, responsible for ensuring their survival, I've had tremendous influence on the wires that have built the brains that perceive their world and create continuous predictions about what they expect to happen in it. They've had that influence on me as well. In very real ways, we've constructed each other. Our relationship is intersubjective, like an ecology. Every interaction is so deeply reliant on what goes on *between* us, and what *has* gone on between us, that it is

impossible to find the lines that create the boundaries where one ends and the other begins. It is impossible to disentangle all the threads. Even so, our stories are our own. Supporting children to grow as themselves means being able to see them as the protagonists of their own life and learning.

Preparing Ourselves to Pay Attention to Connections *and* Interconnections

Preparing for story workshop is an intentional effort to create conditions in which we can heighten our awareness of and care for the ecosystem in which our relationships and children's stories will thrive. In the following example, Kerry was working with second graders who were creating stories that invited them to represent themselves descriptively. A passing exchange between Kerry and a young writer provides a glimpse into the intersubjective construction of meaning that even small moments hold.

A child named Starr told Kerry that her character would be "crazy" because that was what she (Starr) was like. Kerry had noticed that word being used by other children, so she playfully asked for more information. "I noticed that August chose crazy for himself, too. You and August aren't the same! How is your crazy different than his?"

Caroline prepared to observe carefully what happens as the children engage in the experience she has prepared for them.

Starr considered this for a moment and replied, "Well . . . I'm vicious."

It was hard for Kerry not to laugh. She said, "Starr, when I hear the word *vicious*, I think of someone who is trying to hurt someone else. That doesn't make me think of you! Can I make a suggestion?" Starr said she could. "Do you mean feisty?"

Starr smiled and excitedly said, "Yes! That's it. I'm feisty!"

This unplanned encounter was packed with adult decisions

that created conditions for Starr and her classmates to serve their own stories in the company of an adult who did not feel the need to relinquish her own. In this small moment, Kerry found an opportunity to respond to what Starr needed when Starr needed it. She told Starr what she had noticed, which is different from telling Starr what she knew. Though she knew Starr's choice of the word *vicious* was inaccurate, Kerry asked permission to help her revise her idea. Starr agreed. And their partnership resulted in a delightful discovery for them both. Starr added a word to her vocabulary, filled with relationship and shared meaning.

Preparing Ourselves to Listen for Things We Don't Yet Imagine

Resilience, imagination, voice, emotional literacy, and meaning are all contingent on the experiences we encounter within that intersubjective ecology of relationship—and, in a book focused on learning to write, it seems wise to remember that compelling writing is contingent on all of those things. Good spelling doesn't get you there on its own. When adults prepare for exchanges supportive of both identity and intellect, children achieve academically because they learn to value the academic as a set of tools useful and necessary to construct and express deeper meaning.

Relationships can be produced in small moments, way up close, as with Kerry and Starr or Caroline and Stella, or more distantly, as with the child who played with blocks and a question offered in the environment their teacher prepared. The pattern common to these stories involves an adult who sees their role as facilitator, nurturer, listener, and guide—someone who values the child as the protagonist of their learning and their story but who also understands that they have important roles to play in one another's stories.

Hana is prepared with tools to capture what she observes the children say and do. In the videos related to this chapter, you can listen to Hana discuss the way that she uses these observations to prepare for future experiences that support the growth of the children's stories.

Classroom culture is reliant on the story teachers tell themselves about who children are, what they can do, and what school is for. That amounts to an effort to make the invisible visible. In the foreword to Cobb's *Ecology of Imagination in Childhood*, Shaun McNiff writes, "We are so limited by *the way* we think about things, the habits of schooling and psychology, that we cannot see the riches that wait for us if we can begin to reframe how we look at the world" (1993, ix). In Eli's letter to her teacher at the top of this chapter, we see how quickly the habits of schooling take hold as she wrestles with the dissonance she feels between what she imagines a teacher is and does and what she sees Kimie doing. Kimie asks questions. She invites reflection. She does everything with the children. Is that still teaching? McNiff goes on,

Opal School staff meeting

"The child's openness to the world and wonder at what exists *outside the self* instigate creative action" (xi). As Eli wondered at the meaning of *teacher* through her experience with Kimie, we marvel at her insight, but we also see something we might have missed if we hadn't been listening. Somewhere between Eli's words and our old habits and assumptions, we find new territory to explore.

In the limitless ways in which children see the world, we have a chance to cross boundaries we've learned to believe are solid. Impenetrable. Very often, our education systems call on us to shut children's ideas down in order to push our version of the world on them. McNiff writes that teachers "give out information and students give it back to them. During the process, transformation of any kind is considered an incorrect distortion. No wonder the subject and methods of imagination are not taught in school. They contradict the foundations of the enterprise" (1993, xiii). Teachers can imagine the impossible and then head that way alongside the children, who already know how to get there. We can *believe* that the ways in which children reach out to the world at the same time reflect back to them who they are in the world. We can raise our awareness of what we're ensuring that they'll *see*. Teachers can prepare themselves to step into a classroom in which the uncertainty and complexity of the ecology that defines any relationship can be embraced and explored with vulnerability, curiosity, and courage. That becomes possible by starting with clear intentions—an important exercise in self-efficacy for teachers.

Preparing Ourselves with Intention

To prepare for story workshop and all the other content the teachers are excited to explore with children, before the school year begins, they take time to set clear intentions and make them visible. Teachers work together to consider the terrain that lies ahead, what they know about the children (personally and developmentally), and what relevant things are going on in the world or in the community. Teams meet several times together to discuss patterns and connections they see in all of these things and to brainstorm their hopes and goals for their year. As they clarify these intentions, they make projections about the content they intend to investigate together with the children.

Teachers revisit these long-term projections regularly throughout the year as they develop shorter-term intentions monthly, weekly, and daily.

We have developed a set of planning tools to support your thinking as you build this habit of setting intentions, making observations, and engaging in reflection over days, weeks, and months. They are available to download in the Online Resources and include the following:

- *Yearlong Planning Guidelines (Online Resource 2.1)*: This tool provides guiding questions to help you develop intentions for your year and write a letter of intent. (See the next section for an example.)

- *Unit of Study Planning Guidelines (Online Resource 2.2)*: This is a tool to develop a unit of study for use in story workshop. Some teachers choose to work with units of study such as those suggested by Lucy Calkins or Katie Wood Ray. Story workshop doesn't rely on this practice, but it also doesn't need to conflict with it. This tool will help you integrate these structures.

- *Weekly Intentions Guidelines (Online Resource 2.3) and Daily Planning Guidelines (Online Resource 2.4)*: These tools can support your thinking about both weekly and daily planning.

In Video 2.3, you can listen in on a teacher planning meeting as teachers work to make sense of the relationship between daily and long-term intentions.

Writing a Letter of Intent

Letters of intent are written to share with families and to be revisited by teachers over the school year. The letters help teachers focus, think big, foster genuine connections between the children and the curriculum, and stay accountable to the school and the district without predetermining all the pathways. Here is what an intention letter focused on literacy to kindergarten and first-grade families might sound like:

> Dear Families,
>
> We see children as authors—born to share their stories and listen to the stories of others. Children are literate beings long before they learn to read and write conventionally. They are reading the world

Video 2.3 Planning for Story Workshop: Team Meeting

See page ix on how to access this video.

from the moment they are born; they are working to make sense of their experiences in relationship with the people in their lives. This matters because the process of learning to read and write is a naturally compelling one that must begin with them—with their ideas, feelings, and stories. School will be a place where we support children to develop the tools they need to tell their stories well and to find out more about what matters to them, about what they want to say, and about how they want to say it.

This year a big idea we'll be exploring is our relationship to the natural world.

We plan to explore this relationship by taking advantage of the natural world just outside our classroom doors. One goal and expectation for our students is to develop an understanding of our interdependent relationship with the natural world. With this goal in mind, we wonder:

> *How might nurturing our relationship with the*
> *natural world support empathy and agency?*

Inside this big question live smaller questions that are specific to literacy:

- How will our relationship with the natural world help us learn more about ourselves and one another? What new connections will we uncover? What ways will we find to share what we are learning with an audience outside our classroom walls?

- How will the stories we tell shape our relationship with the natural world? With each other? How will those stories help us find out more about what we care about as a community?

- In what ways will our work this year compel us to act with compassion and seek change? How do stories help people make change?

These questions will guide our work together as we explore, discover, and reflect. All along the way, children will be crafting their own stories and learning to work effectively with print as both readers and writers. We look forward to sharing many windows into the children's and teachers' learning experiences and the evolving theories we are constructing together. We look forward to connecting with you about these ideas, too!

Warmly,
Kerry

Planning for the First Day

Following is an example of how a teacher might use the Daily Planning Guidelines (Online Resource 2.4) to prepare for the first day of kindergarten. A second example is available in Online Resource 2.5.

Daily Planning Guidelines

Sample First-Day Plan: *A Focus on Finding and Sharing Stories*

Preparation

- ☞ **Intention:** I want children to know that this is a place where we tell stories. Because of this, I plan to begin by inviting the children to think about, find, and share stories. I want to find out more about who they are, what they love, and experiences they may have had. I believe I can support children as authors by encouraging them to recognize all the stories they already have. I can encourage them by supporting them to know that the real-life experiences they've had often become great stories. I can also begin to nurture connections and develop a culture of a community of authors by inviting them to hear one another's stories.

- ☞ **Setup and materials:** I will want to provide materials that I think might wake up memories. For example, small trays or a sensory table with sand, shells, and pieces of driftwood may be one experience for students to explore. Another may be a space with tempera paint and sunflowers to observe and inspire as they paint. I also want to provide some materials that are open-ended. I will have loose-parts collage, watercolor painting, and blank small books with pens and colored pencils also available.

- ☞ **Text:** *The Big Big Sea*, by Martin Waddell, because it is a short, simple story that, because we live by the sea, I predict these particular children will find connections with.

- ☞ **Documentation:** I will observe how children approach this experience. Will they already view themselves as authors with stories to tell and jump right into this invitation? Will they be more hesitant and seem unsure of what I mean by "finding stories"? I'll pay attention to how the children are using the materials, what language and stories are coming up for them as they play, and the ways in which they are connecting with their peers. I will have my journal and camera as tools for documenting what I see happening during story creation. I will also audio-record the provocation and story sharing so I can go back and listen to what students shared.

Provocation

I plan to begin by saying to children, "One of the things you might not know about me yet is that I love stories! I have found that stories live everywhere! I want to read you a short story that reminded me of a trip I took to the beach with my son. The book is called *The Big Big Sea* and it's by Martin Waddell." I predict that if the beach doesn't inspire them there will be plenty of opportunities for them to make connections with the relationships in this story. After reading, I will say, "Do any of you have connections to this story? What does it make you think of?" As they share, I'll comment on how the connections they are sharing to the book are stories, too.

Invitation and Negotiation

I'll say, "Look around the room and notice all the materials available to you. Today you're going to get a chance to use those materials in the classroom to find or remember a story. What stories can you find or share as you explore the materials in the classroom?" I'll have a list of materials available written or drawn on the board and write children's names underneath as they share where they want to start to find or tell a story.

Story Creation

As I observe, I will be listening and documenting with my camera and notebook. Today, I hope to check in with as many children as I can, begin to build relationships, and get peeks into how they approach this invitation. I'll be working to communicate that this is a place where their ideas matter. As I observe I'll be asking myself: "Who are these children? What do they love and care about? What experiences have they had? How do they approach this invitation? What evidence can I find that they already view themselves as authors? When and where are they seeking opportunities to share their stories with peers?" I'll ask the children: "What stories are you finding as you explore the materials in the classroom? What does this material make you think of? What do you love to do? Tell me something about yourself."

Story Sharing

Because my intention for today is to learn more about these particular children and because I want to support them to get to know one another better, we will spend story sharing time sharing sneak peeks of the ideas for stories that they found today. I'll ask questions like: "Who found an idea for a story they want to share?" and "Who heard an idea for a story that a friend found?" I'll also continue to use this time to have them seek connections between one another and invite them to show a connection hand signal if they have a connection to what someone else shares. I'll also reflect back to them what felt good about the workshop: their focus, the sharing they did with one another, how they took care of the materials, and so on, in order to support the building of these expectations moving forward. We will focus on stories; then I'll help them learn some of our cleanup routines and we will practice.

As I get ready for tomorrow, I will spend some time jotting down my thoughts, observations, and questions in my journal.

All of these planning tools invite as much or as little detail as you need to write in order to move into your work with the children and their families. Some days you'll find that it helps to plan with the level of detail here; this is often especially true on the first day! Other days, once you have internalized the guiding questions and made them a habitual way of thinking, you'll develop shorthand versions that suit your unique needs.

Preparing Tools for Documentation: Capturing the Cycle of Observation and Reflection

You probably have noticed how the planning tools introduced in the previous section are circular. Not only do they nest inside one another, but they end by sending you back to the beginning. None can be started without reflection on context or on prior experience, and none is finished without further reflection that helps us decide on further action. This is because, even as teachers, we experience the world as we experience it. Even when we implement curriculum that was created somewhere else by someone else, we are influenced by our own particular view of things. Lisa Barrett explains, "Your perceptions are so vivid and immediate that they compel you to believe that you experience the world as it is, when you actually experience a world of your own construction" (2018, 86). In other words, perception is a story we tell. Our future actions are influenced by the world we've constructed, whether we're aware of it or not. What any of us learns is not only influenced by, but wholly reliant on, what we explore and the way we explore it. When adults take responsibility for the relationship between this ecology and the child's world making, they can take advantage of the power they have to create the conditions in which children can explore, play, and learn.

As we get older and have more experiences, we rely more on prediction and less on exploration. We don't lose our capacity to play, but we rely on it less to help us navigate the world. We have more certainties and ask fewer questions. An important part of the preparation phase for adults is to create conditions for themselves to wake up that playful part of their brain so they can be more curious about the children and the way they see the world. Reflection is the practice that supports this awakening. Teachers, like any people during waking hours, continually make split-second decisions. As I discussed in the previous chapter, these decisions are based on predictions that are a primal function of our brain. It is difficult to identify the ways in which our perceptions influence our assumptions and behavior. It is the inherent uncertainty in this truth that makes the false promise of "teacher-proof" curriculum seem enticing. We marginalize imagination for the same reason—on the hope that if we can develop a tool that takes the human out of teachers and the children they teach, everything could be much less messy. In our attempt to make learning in school less messy, we've made a big mess of a lot of other things. We've made a world that has largely forgotten the power of our creative birthright—of play, imagination, and story, the very tools we rely on for innovation, for empathy, and for compassion.

> "Seeing is an achievement, not merely a task. It is the result of making sense of a part of the world."
>
> —Elliot Eisner, *The Arts and the Creation of Mind* (2002, 12)

Documentation as a Tool for Awareness, Reflection, and Perceptual Change

The use of tools such as cameras, journals, and audio-recording devices creates a way to slow down after the fact, to reflect on a collection of artifacts in order to look at what we perceived happened through new frames. Neuroscientist Beau Lotto writes, "What your perceptual history of reality gives your brain are **reflexive assumptions** manifest in the functional architecture of the brain with which you perceive the here and now. The assumptions determine what we think and do, and help us to predict what to do next" (2017, 149). These assumptions are neither good nor bad. They just are. But they are powerful and they are consequential and possibly even dangerous when we haven't taken the time to consider the risks in assuming that red means the same thing in your head and in mine. Documentation practices help us become more aware of our assumptions. As we become more aware of our assumptions—even as we become more aware that we *make* assumptions—we become open to more possibility. Where there is more possibility, there is less bias.

Using the Tools of Teacher Research to Slow Down, Pay Attention, and Shift Perspectives

In 1930, author Laura Riding wrote a letter to an eight-year-old friend that included this insight: "People are by themselves in being themselves, but together with everyone and everything else in being everything. And this is what makes a world" (in Popova 2017). The environment we experience, including the other people we find there, is what we use to create ourselves. This is an active process. We are not simply observers of an objective world that spins us around the sun. Our perceptions are an ever-growing collection of experiences we categorize and organize and write into the story we tell about who we are.

In our classrooms and in our lives, we are all in such a hurry so often, so caught up in our own stories, that it can be difficult to ensure that we are building shared meaning together. As teachers, it is important to create ways to slow down, and the process of documentation is an important part of this effort. In order to invite these perceptual shifts, it's helpful to prepare yourself with the tools of teacher research. These include cameras and journals, audio-recording devices (often phone or tablet apps), and a variety of planning and reflection tools that you revise over time through the process of research and as you continually learn more about individual needs and preferences.

Tools of Teacher Research

▶ a journal you love
▶ a pen you love
▶ a camera
▶ a recording device—both audio and video
▶ an app like AudioNote, Notes, or Notability to support transcription and annotation

These tools allow us to engage in a process of documenting what happens in our classrooms and open us to shifts in our perceptions, make us more aware of our assumptions, and help us see things as if they could be otherwise. A practice of documentation does several things:

- It captures meaningful activity, ideas, questions, and responses that we often miss in the moment.

- It expands awareness, helping us be more wide-awake in our practice.

- It tickles imagination and provokes curiosity.

- It supports us to give children space to do what they're doing while we observe them.

- It sends a clear message to children that they are worthy of observation and we are curious about their process.

- It slows us down.

- It helps us focus on children's strengths and create artifacts of authentic assessment.

The tool Using Documentation to Inform Practice (shown here and in Online Resource 2.6) is intended to support the development of a practice of documentation in your setting.

Using Documentation to Inform Practice

Step 1: Ground Yourself

Ground yourself in your stated intentions. Reread your letter if you have one. Take a few minutes to jot them down if you haven't considered them yet.

Step 2: Prepare

- Either choose a focus for your observation (What are you most curious about? What do you want to gather more information about?) or decide that you are going to observe with an open mind and see what emerges.

- Consider how you will position yourself to observe what you hope to see.

- Decide what tools you will need and have them ready.

- Consider asking a volunteer, an assistant, or a colleague to support your class so you can focus on observing.

Step 3: Observe

- Try to capture your notes as literally as possible, without too much judgment or critique.

- Write down exactly what children say. Consider audio recording to augment your notes.

- Try to capture what you see. Use sketching if you are comfortable.

- Take photographs to support your memory and to provide insight later.

Step 4: Interpret and Speculate

- During your planning time, look over your data (the artifacts you collected during your observation).

- What do you notice? What patterns do you see? Write down your thoughts without critique.

- What connections are you making between what you observed and what you believe about teaching and learning?

- What evidence do you see that supports your interpretation?

- What surprises, gaps, or confusion do you experience?

- What speculations does the data motivate?

Step 5: Consider Implications

- What does your interpretation of your data suggest about what you should do next?

- Does the evidence suggest that you are headed in a direction you intended to go? Does it suggest that you need to alter your course in one way or another?

Step 6: Engage with Colleagues

- Organize your data and your reflections and share them with colleagues.

- Invite your colleagues to share their interpretations and speculations.

- Brainstorm implications or possibilities for next steps.

- Generate new questions.

- Consider creating a shared archive of documentation (Google and Evernote are good options, but there are many others) so that you can collaborate when you don't have time to meet.

Preparing the Classroom to Welcome Story

In story workshop, the intentional organization of the environment and materials invites children to have opportunities throughout the day to explore the classroom with everything they bring—their bodies, their curiosities, their cares, and their imaginations. Small spaces within the classroom are designed to inspire imagination and curiosity. Time is organized so that the children are able to work and play within these spaces. Many kinds of materials are available for exploration, play, and discovery.

What We Feel Is What We Learn: Preparing the Aesthetic Dimension

We try to prepare the environment with high attention to its aesthetic quality. If the idea of

aesthetic feels alienating, perhaps it helps to think of its opposite, anesthetic, which is excellent in the dentist's office but not so much for learning. If our goal is to intensify our power of perception—because perception includes all the tools we use to construct meaning—we want to design environments that heighten feeling rather than numb it. It might also help to consider this: "Every concept you have ever learned includes the state of your body at the time of learning. Some concepts involve a lot of feeling, such as 'Sadness,' and others have less, such as 'Plastic Wrap,' but they're always in relation to the same body. So every categorization you construct—about objects in the world, other people, purely mental concepts like 'Justice,' and so on—contains a little bit of you" (Barrett 2018, 191).

What we feel when we learn something becomes a part of what we've learned. The things we offer children to explore, and the materials we offer them to express the stories that are born of exploration, not only constrain or expand what is possible for them now but also give shape to what becomes possible for them as they go forward. Immordino-Yang writes, "Emotion may play a vital role in helping children decide when and how to apply what they have learned in school to the rest of their lives" (2016, 32). Because we are defined by our own interactions within the ecology available to us, our capacity for agency is inherent to our powers of perception. That agency is story. Our classrooms can become environments where we endeavor to strengthen narrative agency in young children. Our classrooms can become the kind of places that children explore as they might a forest or a tide pool. Imagine how important this might be for children who have had little opportunity to explore the equivalent of either! In the classroom, we have the particular advantage of being able to intentionally create an environment that strengthens each individual's agency through story and, in so doing, invites interrogation by others who don't see the world as they do. We want to design an ecology that is healthy and thriving because of its diversity.

Consider the contrast between the classroom environments in Figures 2.1 and 2.2. One is designed to reduce perceptual volume. One is designed to turn

Figure 2.1 Opal School classroom for ages 6–8

Figure 2.2 Anesthetic classroom environment

it up. One is designed for transmission. One is designed for construction. One is designed to prioritize answers. One is designed for big questions. One is designed to reduce uncertainty. One is designed to learn how to manage ourselves within it. Learning happens in both classrooms. If we believe that our task is to take information we hold in the teacher's manual and migrate it to the heads of the students, it makes sense to turn down the volume on all the other possible distractions. But because our sensory systems continue to work in whatever environment we encounter—because we are making meaning all the time—we believe the world we experience is as it is. Which world do you want children to believe in?

Try This: *Notice How Your Classroom Makes You Feel*

Reflect on this question: How should learning feel in a body?

Stand in your classroom before the children arrive.

How do you feel?

What revisions might you make to your environment that could promote the feelings you think learning should feel like?

Once you've done an initial exploration of how your classroom feels, grab your notebook and spend some time looking around your classroom. Jot notes about what you notice. How does the space communicate an attitude of care and attention? Does it engage the senses and invite possibilities?

Look over your notes and decide on one change you'd like to make to your classroom environment that you predict will further support children to find, tell, and share their stories.

If you would like to take a deeper dive into the aesthetic quality of your classroom environment, see Online Resource 2.7.

Organizing Materials

There are as many ways to organize materials as there are materials to organize! The most important reason to organize thoughtfully is that it communicates care. Care supports relationship and it associates feeling good with learning—an association that deserves intentional nurturing. Children quickly learn to manage the organization of many materials when adults take time to thoughtfully organize what's available.

It is often a good idea to introduce children to materials slowly because it gives you time to support processes for cleanup and care as you go along. Place materials you want children to use within their reach so they can access them and care for them independently. You may wish to put some materials into a rotation and have some that are always available. Experiment with what works for you and seek input from colleagues when you get stuck!

The images on these next two pages are intended to support your imagination for possibilities. At Opal School, for a long time, a parent brought teachers the empty plastic containers that held suet she left for birds in her yard. They were the perfect size for small loose parts. Most of the collections we have at Opal School, and the containers that hold them, are full of their own stories—and they cost next to nothing.

Quality brushes are a good investment.

Many materials can be found and organized in aesthetically pleasing ways at very little cost.

A collection of natural materials, many collected and dried by the children

Variation in the block area

Organization supports care.

Watercolor supplies

Wire

Construction materials

Potter's clay and modeling clay

Torn paper

For further reading, try these resources:

- *The Language of Art*, by Ann Pelo
- *In the Spirit of the Studio* (both editions), edited by Lella Gandini, Lynn Hill, Louise Cadwell, and Charles Schwall
- *Bringing Reggio Emilia Home*, by Louise Cadwell
- *Designs for Living and Learning*, by Deb Curtis and Margie Carter
- *Inspiring Spaces for Young Children*, by Jessica DeViney, Sandra Duncan, Sara Harris, Mary Ann Rody, and Lois Rosenberry
- *Beautiful Stuff! Learning with Found Materials*, by Cathy Weisman Topal and Lella Gandini

Try This: *Make Your Own Loose-Parts Collection*

You can find loose parts almost anywhere! Start by looking in your own house or yard for reusable or recyclable materials. Things like screws, nuts, bolts, recycled lids, scraps of fabric, corks, ribbon, yarn, beads, old jewelry, and natural materials will get you started in building your own collection. Look for small, clear containers that make it easy to organize, see, and access the materials. I keep a bag in my house to collect interesting odds and ends that might otherwise be tossed away and bring the bag to school to sort and organize when it's full. To grow your collection, you might consider asking the families you work with to donate their own interesting found and (clean) reusable materials.

What Materials Should You Use?

When it comes to collecting materials for use in story workshop, the possibilities are practically endless. The materials that become a part of your story workshop should be open to interpretation, highly flexible, and both familiar and surprising; they should invite mark making of many kinds, offer experience with movement and impermanence, be responsive to the children and reflect the identity of their community and place, and bring a sense of beauty and inspiration to the environment.

Making Friends with Materials

I know it isn't common that teachers have much experience using a wide variety of materials or art media in a way that makes it natural to use them in the classroom. Luckily, prior experience isn't really necessary. But materials are a critical part of the story workshop process, and before you offer materials to children, it's a good idea to have played with them yourself. For this reason, as a feature in most chapters, I'll invite you to set up and explore materials alone or with a group of colleagues.

When children are first introduced to any material, they benefit from time to play, explore, and generally mess around in order to discover the qualities that distinguish one from another. We have found the same to be true with adults. Having an opportunity to do this allows us to become more familiar with a material and to develop an understanding of what each material can do. We call this kind of experience an *affordances study*. This first invitation can be used with any material you have on hand, and we encourage you to do it with any you intend to (or already) use with children. This first materials exploration and reflection invites you to engage in your own affordances study. In later chapters, I'll invite you to use materials as tools for thinking and reflection, but each time you use a new material, it helps to return to an affordances study.

Materials Exploration: Watercolors

⚐ **Materials needed:** watercolor palette, crayons, watercolor paper (preferred), one or two paintbrushes, dishes for water, paper towel, a twelve-by-eighteen-inch piece of colored paper to define a work area and protect the table

⚐ **Preparing your environment:** See the following sketch for a suggested organization of materials.

⚐ **Getting started:** Prepare your work space and start exploring. As you play with this material, pay attention. What can this material do? Notice that this is a different question from *What can you do with the material?* With the focus on the material itself, rather than on your work product, what do you notice?

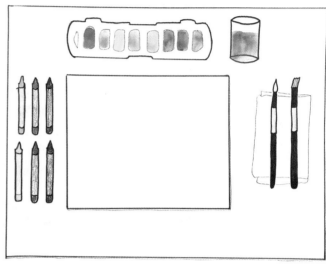

As you play, make a list of the different things that you are discovering these materials can do—on their own and together.

If you are engaging in this process with colleagues, compare your lists. What did your colleagues discover about what these materials can do that you might add to your list? Or continue to ask yourself, "What else can they do?" What words do you need to describe the things they can do? Do you need to create words for your discoveries? Feel free to label your work directly instead of creating a separate list.

⚐ **Reflecting:**

◆ What do you notice about the unique gifts of each material?

◆ What are the similarities? What are the differences? What surprised you?

◆ How does taking time to explore these affordances increase the opportunity you have to express your ideas with them?

◆ What affordances study would benefit the children you are working with currently?

Action Steps: Enrich Your Story Workshop Practice

🍂 If you are inspired by the beauty of the environments in the images in this book, create an organization system for the materials in your classroom that is aesthetically pleasing and teach the children how to manage it. Notice the differences this makes in the way you and the children feel in the environment and about the work you do together.

🍂 If you are curious about the power of the aesthetic dimension, reflect on the connections between beauty, relationship, and nonviolence. Keep track of the questions you have about these connections and the implications they hold for your work with children within environments intended for learning. To support your reflection and research, read essays by Vea Vecchi, Maxine Greene, John Dewey, or Elaine Scarry.

🍂 If you are intrigued by the neuroscience of perception, dive into Beau Lotto's book *Deviate* (2017). Take notes as you consider the implications for your work with young children. How might his research influence the choices you make in your classroom?

EDUCATOR INTERVIEW:
EVERYONE IS ABLE TO TELL A STORY

Excerpted from an interview with Alana Tesan, kindergarten teacher Annieville Elementary School, Delta School District, British Columbia

ANNIEVILLE ELEMENTARY is a public school serving middle-class families with lots of ethnic diversity. Once I started doing story workshop, I felt like the children were finally allowed to reveal themselves, like reveal the inner parts of them that maybe they couldn't [before], based on the box that we are always trying to fit them in at school. Story workshop allowed them to tell stories about themselves that we may otherwise never know. One of the things that I like about story workshop is that there's an entry point for everyone. I have a student this year who came to kindergarten already reading and writing. He can play during story workshop, and he can also write independently. The other kids that come to kindergarten not even knowing the names of the letters in their own name are still able to play and tell their story—and feel successful. I had a little girl who moved here from Korea just a couple of days before school started. She speaks no English at all, but she can tell a story. She can create. She started learning the words for things, and her stories at the beginning were like, "Rainbow, flower, me." By spring, she was telling stories in sentences. Her ideas are usually about mermaids and all kinds of amazing imaginary things. They all live inside her, and because of the language barrier, I would never have known that about her without story workshop.

I remember setting up my very first provocation to invite the children to tell a story, and I set it up so nicely that no one wanted to touch it. And I realized that I had taken it too far. Even though I said to the kids, "You can move things around; change it however you want," it was too perfect. So now when I set up, I don't set it up in the sense that I'm starting the story. Because it's not my story to tell. I invite them to find a story in the materials or tell a story that lives in them or their imagination. I'm just providing the materials to do it.

One thing I would say to another teacher if they were asking me about story workshop is that the challenging behaviors that usually arise are gone. The poking of the other kids, and the running around the classroom, and all the things that we are trying to not have kids do because it's school and we all have to live together in this same community are gone. That behavior management doesn't exist in the same way in story workshop, I think because of the fact that it's all about them. It's their story, their idea. They are deciding what materials to use. They are deciding what words to use.

I think everything we do at school can revolve around story. So by opening up the world of story to children, I think you get to know them better. You listen to their conversations and their stories and you find out what they're interested in, which, for me, guides my practice. I think that it also gives children ownership over their own learning and pride in the fact that this has come from them. It's not teacher-directed or scripted. There is no right answer. It comes right from their soul. It comes from their heart and who they are and the things that they're interested in. Everyone is able to tell a story.

"A story is powerful because after you read it,
the story becomes a part of you."

—Stella (age 9)

CHAPTER THREE

Provocation: Presenting Content to Be Learned

Provocation is the beginning of a story workshop session, offering a proposal to children to engage, sustain, and extend their interests and curiosity as they begin the workshop. Here's a little sneak peek into a provocation in a combined kindergarten and first-grade class in early December (see also Video 3.1):

> **Sarah** (teacher)**:** Why do people create stories?
>
> **Millie:** Just if you want to make a friend with someone that you don't know that lives way in a different country.
>
> **Sarah:** So you think that sharing stories about your life could help you make a friend? To connect with somebody else?
>
> **Simon:** Oh sure!
>
> **Sarah:** Who can add on to that?

Video 3.1
Provocation:
Children Ages 5–7

Video 3.2
Provocation:
Children Ages 3–5

See page ix on how to access these videos.

Millie: It's important so other people don't ask too much questions about you.

Evelyn: Though some people like being asked questions and they still write stories. Like I like being asked questions and I write. In fact, I published two books last year about myself.

An Important Note About Picture Books

The use of high-quality children's literature of many kinds is a daily part of school and almost always during story workshop. Although, for copyright reasons, we had to remove books from all of the images printed here, rest assured that beautiful and intentionally chosen picture books blanket classrooms engaged in this practice. We give much care to ensure that any art visible within the classroom represents a strong and joyful image of diverse children, cultures, and families. Children absorb a great deal of meaning from those choices and we are accountable for them. We have included a list of some of our favorite pieces of literature to inspire story workshop online. (See Online Resource 3.1.)

What Is Provocation? Telling Is Not Teaching

Consider the ways in which the children in Sarah's class (see dialogue that opens this chapter and Video 3.1) quickly become a part of the action. Sarah asks an open-ended question, listens to the children's ideas, and encourages them to add on. In so doing, she orchestrates a shared event, nurturing the ecology.

People are not receivers. People are thinkers, makers, and connectors. Here is some of what we know about that:

- **Sensory perception** is what prompts us to make predictions. The learning brain wonders: *What in my environment has captured my attention?*

- **Making connections** is how we learn new things. The learning brain wonders: *How does this new information reinforce or challenge what I already know?*

- ✏ **Emotion** is a concept that explains the state of our bodies, built of experience *in* our bodies. The learning brain wonders: *What is happening in the rest of my body as I make connections and predictions?*

- ✏ **Story** is the thought structure we use to make meaning of our encounters with the world. The learning brain wonders: *How will I organize this experience so I can make sense of it?*

- ✏ **Language** is a means for expressing our stories. The learning brain wonders: *What images and words can I attach to this experience that will give outer form to my inner world?*

Once we have prepared an environment designed to be supportive of and compatible with what we currently understand about the biology of human cognition, perception, and communication, and we have prepared ourselves with a playful and curious mindset, we are ready to join the children.

A provocation invites children to slow down, look closely, and pay attention to their own view of things.

Provocation Is an Alternative to Transmission

Provocation is a whole-group gathering facilitated by the teacher, who is intentional about drawing out the children's unique predictions and connections. It is a time devoted to the lively exploration of the complexity that is alive within the relationships that make up their community of story makers, storytellers, and listeners, one of whom happens to be a grown-up with extra years of interesting and relevant information to share but who is aware that they do not see the world as the children do. Teachers plan for provocation knowing that children must bring forward what they already know in order to learn something new.

Learning is a creative, collaborative, and social endeavor, simultaneously emotional and cognitive. There is no difference, no separation, between what happens in our mind and in our body. Ever. Provocation is designed to embrace that powerful truth, to invite it in and to explore it as a vital contributor to the stories we create. We refer to provocation as a specific part of the structure of a story workshop session but also as the experience teachers facilitate during that time. If you are familiar with writing workshop, you'll see obvious parallels between provocations and minilessons, including the fact that they both ready the children to use their independent work time constructively.

During provocation, a teacher may plan to use a provocation *or* a minilesson, and sometimes they'll use both. Minilessons and provocations are similar in practice but derive from varied intentions. (See tools for intention setting in "Preparing Ourselves with Intention" in Chapter 2, page 42, and in the online resources.) In this chapter, I'll develop the distinctions in order to support you to choose with intention from this broad range of possibilities for getting started with story workshop each day.

During story creation, a provocation invites a child to use collage materials to find a story.

Writing Workshop Connection: *Minilessons*

Typically, writing workshop begins with a teacher-directed mini-lesson. Based on observations of children at work, the teacher designs a short (five- to twenty-five-minute) lesson to begin the workshop. Minilessons support product and process. They might be focused on craft, convention, agreements such as the kind of noise level writers need in order to focus or where to put finished work, or the use of technical skills such as the proper operation of a stapler. Minilessons also include guidance for giving and receiving feedback or how to let people know you'd like to share your work. This is a powerful structure that supports young writers to develop strong skill and strategy as well as to nurture the community to work together pro-ductively as authors. Because there are so many high-quality resources to support teachers in creating and implementing minilessons, I keep the focus here on creating and using provocations.

What stories live inside of a **smell?** How can you capture this with these materials?

Can you find a story in the sand?

Provocations Invite Children to Play with Ideas

A provocation starts as a kind of prediction that a teacher makes—a hunch about what will spark and sustain the children's curiosity and engagement. It is intended to support the teacher's ongoing sequence of observation and reflection followed by decision making in a way that Loris Malaguzzi once described as a kind of "ball toss" (in Edwards, Gandini, and Nimmo 2015, 14). The teacher tosses something (an idea, a question, a challenge) to the children, and the children catch and toss back (curiosity, more ideas and questions,

enthusiasm)—or they don't. When they don't, the teacher makes adjustments in order to allow for and to encourage an extension of the game. The teacher learns to experience moments when the ball seems to get dropped with an attitude of curiosity. This ball toss is a process of inquiry for everyone involved. Teachers might ask: "If the children aren't engaged, what's another way that I can toss this ball so that they are more likely to toss it back?" The analogy of the ball toss works well for provocation because it is built on the assumption that children *want to play*. They want to be engaged, to tell stories, to connect, and to belong. They are curious, creative, and competent.

Each day during preparation, teachers must make decisions. What is the most reasonable next step? What do I predict will create the most engaged conversation between me and the children and the content?

The chart in Figure 3.1 demonstrates a possible use of the Weekly Intentions Guidelines (see Chapter 2, page 42, and Online Resource 2.3) to develop plans for a provocation that is responsive to observations but also true to intentions and learning goals. This teacher's intention for the next week or two was to support children in becoming familiar with the genre of literary nonfiction in order to inspire their own writing. Their current content focus in other areas of the curriculum was to explore the topic of forests, and the teacher wanted to invite connections to that content as part of story workshop.

Notice that even though this teacher's intention was to engage children with literary nonfiction, she started by asking the children to consider the various ways they might use writing to share their learning about forests with others. She predicted that by provoking their interest in sharing their learning, she would engage them more deeply in the work going forward, and she thought that the deeper engagement would lead to higher-quality work. She trusted that it was unlikely that the children would name "literary nonfiction" on their own, and she predicted that, by inviting them to generate a list of possibilities, she could later introduce literary nonfiction in a direct way by showing the relationship to their ideas. First they would construct the concept together; then they would name it.

Then, she planned to say something like, "I notice there are so many different ways to write about the forest. You know, there is one genre that combines some of these ideas, and authors use it when they want to combine

Figure 3.1 Sample of a Weekly Intentions Planning Chart

WEEKLY INTENTIONS PLANNING CHART				
	Intention	**Observation**	**Provocation**	**Minilesson**
Day 1	Children will prepare to publish a piece of literary nonfiction in order to support our current project work focus: forests.	Children's engagement in project work would benefit from creating opportunity to communicate what they are learning to an authentic audience.	What are the ways you think we could use writing to help people know more about the important things we're learning about the forest?	
Day 2	Same as above.	Children's list of possibilities for writing include both fiction and non-fiction categories.		Introduce literary nonfiction.
Day 3	Children will begin to identify characteristics of literary nonfiction.	Children are ready to engage with mentor texts.	Read and discuss *The Tree Lady: The True Story of How One Tree-Loving Woman Changed a City Forever* by Hopkins.	Begin making a chart of what the children notice about this genre.
Day 4	Same as above.	Children are eager to find connections.	Read and discuss *Pedal Power: How One Community Became the Bicycle Capital of the World* by Drummond.	Continue the chart.
Day 5	Children will use language in their writing that is indicative of literary nonfiction.	The language in children's initial drafts is a bit dry.	How can materials help you find new language for your piece? What happens if you try working on your piece with a different material? Can you find new ways to say what you mean?	
Day 6	Children will develop effective spelling strategies.	As vocabulary becomes more sophisticated, children are reluctant to "have a go" at spelling words they feel are difficult.	What strategies do you use when you feel stuck on spelling a hard word?	Practice "having a go" at spelling words that seem hard.

some different ways of writing. It's called literary nonfiction. Your list reminds me of that genre." The teacher was tossing the ball so they would play the game with her. She was drawing out their ideas and priming their perception so that the content she wanted them to learn would have a good chance of being perceived as personally meaningful and useful. This is a worthy investment of time.

Speaking of time . . . this is the kind of planning projection a teacher might make when beginning a new focus for story workshop. Based on the actual work, what begins as a six-day plan may change shape or be reordered or take ten days. The teacher can't fill in the observation column ahead of time. The teacher sets intentions, pays attention to what actually happens, and makes decisions responsive to those observations. The ongoing process of observation and reflection is an important part of what happens from one day to the next. Teachers who like to plan in grade-level groups may set intentions together, but

A dramatic play area is a provocation embedded in the story workshop environment. It is an ongoing invitation to find and tell stories.

A teacher uses a photograph of the children at work during story workshop as a provocation for further discussion.

the route to those intentions will vary because the ecology of each particular group is necessarily different. When teachers share documentation as part of the collaborative planning process, they may seek opportunities to bring ideas or other inspiration from one group of children to another to seed connections between groups. The focus on intentions helps teachers support one another to stay committed to a common destination while encouraging one another to travel a unique path.

Provocations Are Always Questions, Even When They Don't Sound Like Questions

A provocation is, essentially, a good question. Sometimes it is asked with words and sometimes it is posed through the design of the environment, or the presentation of materials, or another relevant piece of art or writing, but it always intended to reveal and build links between what the children already know and what we believe they have a right to know. "Good questions reveal and build links in the same way the brain does in order to construct a reality . . . a past we use to perceive in the future . . . out of the objective one that we don't have access to" (Lotto 2017, 197).

Teachers can't deliver objectivity, but they can ensure that what goes on in their classroom is rich with the conditions that are most likely to create the perceptions of, attention to, and engagement with the things teachers intend for children to learn. Zaretta Hammond defines a provocation in this way: "Select an eye-opening quote with strong emotion, a challenging puzzle, an outrageous statement, create a slideshow with powerful images related to the lesson, or show a video clip that arouses emotions. Challenge the dominant culture's worldview or speak to relevant community issues. These types of openings provoke us and create a gentle disequilibrium. These cues not only signal the brain to pay attention but also provide some type of priming that makes the [brain] scan the lesson, reading or discussion of the answer. Wake up the [brain]. . . . Catch them off guard to increase the impact" (2015, 129).

The following story illustrates how the teachers' use of observation, reflection, and questions helped them keep everyone's brain "awake" and supported them to create meaningful provocations for the children (ages three to five).

Pictures of Practice
Asking Questions to Embrace Uncertainty

During fall parent-teacher conferences, many parents shared observations of their children's growing interest in the alphabet and in reading environmental print. Based on these encounters with parents, their own observations of the children, and their curricular intentions, the teachers predicted a study of the alphabet would be a ball the children wanted to catch and were likely to return in an interesting way.

Their first provocation began with a reading of *The City ABC Book*, by Zoran Milich, to the whole group. This alphabet book is made up of a series of black-and-white photographs that somehow feature a letter of the alphabet, embedded within the composition, which has been outlined in red by the author. The teachers had prepared several photographs of familiar places within the classroom, and after reading the book, they asked the children if they could identify hidden letters in the photographs.

Arlo exclaimed, "I can see the letters from right here!" And a chorus of "Me, too!" sprung up all around the circle. This excitement felt like a return of the ball to the teachers. And so the teachers encouraged the game to continue by inviting the children to explore the environment outside their classroom. They challenged the children to search for letters embedded in the environment (like Milich had), not on signs and clothing. One child returned the ball with a suggestion that they bring alphabet charts with them so they could check off the letters as they found them.

The first letters that jumped to their attention were lots of *I*'s, *T*'s, *L*'s, and *O*'s. They were everywhere! They were on the floor, in the windows, in the walls, on door handles. The children kept finding the same few letters over and over again. This wasn't terribly disappointing to the children, but it was frustrating to the teachers, who intended to focus on the whole alphabet and not just a few letters.

The frustration in this challenge was its own kind of ball toss. The teachers wondered how they could help the children see beyond the obvious letters that they found over and over again. So they decided to ask them to look for specific letters.

The children complied and seemed happy enough to continue with the search. However, they had less energy, and the teachers sensed that they had begun looking for what they wanted to see rather than listening for opportunities to make connections to what children already knew. The experience no longer felt like everyone was wide-awake and enjoying a lively game of toss. So the teachers decided to come together to reflect on the work, considering questions such as these:

- What does this project mean to the children?

- How might our agenda be limiting what we are able to learn from the children?

- How might this experience be organized to tell us more about the children's engagement and interest in print and what their questions and curiosities are?

The teachers considered the points along the way where they had felt a ball tossed by the children. They looked over photographs and notes they had taken. They remembered the excitement the children shared as they scanned the visual elements around them. Sometimes the children pointed to textures or other things that were not letters—noticing more and perceiving more in the environment than the teachers and wanting to talk about it. The children seemed to be wondering: "If these aren't letters, then what *are* they?"

The teachers wondered if they could pick up the ball where the most interest was and get their game of toss going again. They considered a new set of questions:

- What if we broadened the scope of our investigation to include other symbols and ways of expressing meaning through line, or color in addition to lines, that result in letters?

- How might this investigation enrich and deepen the original intention to explore the alphabet and environmental print? If we attend to what's not a letter, will the children have a better understanding of what is a letter?

- How might expanding this study, based on observations of these particular children, strengthen their expressive language and vocabulary?

One of the teachers, Kimie, wrote the following reflection as they struggled to find their way forward:

> The possibility of this becoming so much bigger and beyond an alphabet study both excited and scared me. I felt daunted by what it might become and by the open-endedness of it all. Would it become so open that I would lose direction and lose the children's investment and connection? I am so full of uncertainty about my role and how to invite possibilities through this ball toss without letting my agenda take over or losing a focus altogether. I'm so curious what else I need to consider as I move forward and what my colleagues might recommend.

Reflection

Consider the story of the alphabet search through the lens of the three dispositions of world-makers you chose. (See Reflection section in Chapter 1, page 24.) What do you see? What do you wonder?

Thinking in Questions

The uncertainty Kimie describes is necessary to the process, though it's not anyone's favorite part. Uncertainty is uncomfortable for anyone but especially for teachers, whose work is commonly seen as an effort to stomp out uncertainty—to replace not knowing with knowing. But Kimie and her colleagues were doing exactly what they needed to be doing as they worked to merge their intentions for their work and the *actual* children. A reflective and responsive practice is inherently uncertain and, not incidentally, creative. But it is also relational and, therefore, joyful.

The provocation invites children to play with the idea of self and encourages stories from within that context.

Teachers ask questions because questions engage the mind with that gentle disequilibrium that makes us want to resolve it. Our brains are wired to resolve uncertainty (Lotto 2017), so questions alert our perceptions and signal us to pay attention. Questions are the tools of teachers' trade. It is important that teachers learn to use these tools as skillfully and as precisely as a surgeon uses theirs or as an artist uses theirs. If our goal is genuine engagement with intended content, the irony is that we can't rely all the time on asking questions that we already know the answer to about that content. So, this ensures we will find ourselves mucking around in uncertainty.

Good questions are questions that no one yet knows the answer to. Even better questions are those that no one can really ever know the answer to. "Unanswerable questions" (a term coined by Opal School third graders) have the power to invite us into a state of relaxed alertness. The challenge is high but the risk is low: there is no way to be wrong. The uniquely personal connections we make as we puzzle through the unanswerable help coalesce the known and the unknown, binding the world as we perceive it and the others we encounter to our sense of who we are. In the best case, we feel connected. We achieve a sense of belonging. And we want more. School can feel like this.

Caroline observes a small group of
children responding to a provocation
during story creation.

Asking Good Questions

Questions help us build intellectual mus-
cle because this kind of puzzling over the
unanswerable (as long as the stakes are
low) makes us want to keep puzzling. For
these very reasons, unanswerable questions
are a basic ingredient of creating meaningful provocations. These questions don't
have answers. They aren't intended to have
conclusions. They are tossed as an invitation to play and expand the life of the
imagination, to encourage connection, and
to sustain and strengthen curiosity. They
are intended to make it feel good to think
and to think together with people in your
community—so that when we are faced
with not knowing, as we all so frequently
are, we've had practice moving forward
through collaboration and with courage.

The chart in Figure 3.2 explores a
variety of questions that might be asked
during provocation. In the first column, the
questions are those that the teacher already knows the answer to. In practice,
these may be posed as questions or not; the teacher may choose to remind
children that there is an accepted answer to the question and that they feel it
is important for the children to know that particular answer.

Authentic questions are those that the teacher does not know the answer
to and is genuinely curious about. Depending on the intention of the question,
it may frame a minilesson or a provocation. A teacher might ask a question
such as, "What connections do you have to this story?" as an open-ended
way to begin a lesson on the concept of schema through a minilesson or
with the intention to toss a ball to the children, exploring their connections
to a story they have read as an invitation to engage with each other and to

prompt thinking about what they themselves might like to write about. And, of course, it could be both. Authentic questions invite children to share their ideas, interpretations, connections, questions, theories, feelings, and experiences. Authentic questions make space for multiple perspectives and open the door to dialogue.

Unanswerable questions are authentic, but they take the opportunity for dialogue a little further. Unanswerable questions sometimes invite more opportunity for conflict and tension, which is highly valuable within a thought community. In his book *Nonsense*, Jamie Holmes (2016) quotes psychologist Sidney D'Mello, who says, "People come alive when the world breaks down" (170). These tensions and confusions can become a signal within a community of learners that it is time to pay closer attention to what lies beneath the surface.

Figure 3.2 Three Types of Questions

Known (Minilesson)	Authentic (Minilesson or Provocation)	Unanswerable (Provocation)
What is the difference between fiction and nonfiction?	What does this story remind you of?	Where do you find stories?
What are the ways you can end a sentence?	How does punctuation support this author's story?	How do feelings live inside stories?
What is metacognition?	What does it mean to understand?	How does thinking about thinking work inside a storyteller's brain?
What is the difference between *they're, their,* and *there*?	Why do people rely on conventional spelling?	How do writers choose the best words for a story?

All of these kinds of questions have value. The important thing is to know your intentions and then to know how to create and choose questions that will move you toward them. The best way to know whether you're getting there is through an ongoing process of documentation and reflection.

Try This: *Creating Questions*

Think of a topic you are currently exploring with your students or that is of particular interest to you personally. Use the blank chart in Online Resource 3.2 (shown here) to develop questions in each category.

CREATING QUESTIONS CHART		
Known (Minilesson)	Authentic (Minilesson or Provocation)	Unanswerable (Provocation)

There are three types of questions—known, authentic, and unanswerable—all of which have value. The important thing is to know your intentions and then know how to create and choose questions that will move you toward them. Use this form to practice writing each kind of question based on your intentions. After you have written your questions, make a decision about which you predict will best move you toward your intentions.

Introducing Materials to the Children

Children may respond to questions through dialogue, through materials, or through both. Provocation can be a time to support children to use materials to think with, so it is important to take the time to introduce materials to children and give them time to explore them.

The bottom two images illustrate a couple of ways you could ask children questions through materials.

The language we use when we talk about materials is filled with the same attitude of care and attention that goes into the preparation, organization, and presentation of the materials. The words we choose build up concepts that hold possibilities and encouragement to imagine relationships with materials the children may not have considered before. We may refer to a material as a "new friend" that will help us tell our stories, or we may bring the materials ceremoniously to the whole group and reveal them in a special way. When we model a feeling of excitement and enthusiasm for materials and tools of the arts, the children willingly engage in the thrill of expressive and creative possibility along with us.

In addition to dialogue during provocation, children use a wide variety of materials as tools to explore provocations during story creation.

What does red make you think of?

What *red* stories wake up inside of you or come into you?

Pictures of Practice
Introducing Loose-Parts Collage

The following dialogue took place as Caroline introduced materials for loose-parts collage to a group of three- to five-year-old children.

Caroline: Sage, yesterday you were painting and you discovered a story about a unicorn. Did you know that would happen?

Sage: A story just popped out of my head!

Caroline: It was so exciting! I have something else that's really exciting to tell you. [Caroline shifts her voice to a whisper as though she is sharing a great secret with the children.] **Paint is not the only place where you can find stories.**

Will: Stories are everywhere!

Caroline: [Animated and building suspense] **Yes! Did you know that you can also find stories at blocks, like Harrison? He told a dinosaur story last week. Or, you might find a story in clay, like Bella and Fritz. They found a story about a worm family. Now, I want to introduce you to a new material.**

[Caroline stands up to get a few collage materials and a piece of black felt off the table, where they've been organized for use during story creation. Several children cover their eyes in anticipation of a big surprise.

She returns to the circle and places the items carefully on the floor.] **Are you ready to see?**

[The children open their eyes. A few say, "Collage!"]

[Caroline nods her head.] **This is collage, and it's another material where you might find a story today.**

[The children lean forward and peer into the containers.]

Sage: **That green thing, that's a snake.** [Caroline smiles and carefully pulls out the piece Sage is pointing to and places it at the bottom of the black felt.]

Astrid: **The white pompoms could be clouds.** [She picks up a few pompoms and scatters them across the top.]

Julian: **Fire, a nice fire.**

Sage: **With these.** [She picks up shimmery bronze tiles and hands them to Caroline, who places them on the black felt.]

Ravi: [Pointing to blue pompoms] **This can be the sky.**

Marlowe: [Holding up a stick] **This can be a person!**

Julian: [Gathering two more sticks] **Daddy, Mommy, me.**

Sage: [Considering what she knows about Julian] **And he has a little brother, one more.**

Ravi: [Handing Caroline a white pompom] **They're roasting marshmallows.**

Sage: [Picking up another green piece] **This is Mommy snake; this is Baby snake.**

Astrid: **This could be the sun!**

Ravi: **Next to the clouds!**

Caroline: **Who feels ready to try out collage? During story creation today, I wonder what story will pop into your head as you play with collage materials?**

Reflection

How do you see evidence of your three chosen dispositions of world-makers showing up in pictures of practice?

Any materials that you can get your hands on, and organize and care for, are worth introducing to children, who will play with anything they can get their hands on! When their hands are on materials, their minds are, too, and stories will come.

Try This: *Introduce Watercolor to Children*

The introduction of materials can happen during story workshop, but it doesn't have to. I include this invitation to try bringing a new material (or four or five!) to children in this chapter because story creation can't happen without these tools.

Watch Video 3.3, "Introducing Watercolor," and think about these questions:

- How are the materials organized?

- What stands out to you about the language the teachers use to discuss the materials with each other and with the children?

Gather your own collection of watercolor materials—palettes, crayons, pencils, and so on.

Video 3.3 Introducing Watercolor: Children Ages 5–7

See page ix on how to access this video.

Plan to introduce the materials:

- Will you introduce this material to the whole group or a small group?

- When will this introduction take place—during story workshop or another time of day when materials can be available for children to explore?

- What will children need (e.g., placemat, brush, jar with water, blotter or paper towel, watercolor material)? Choose one kind of watercolor to start with: palettes, pencils, crayons, or liquid.

- How will you organize these materials in a way that feels inviting and caring?

- What language will you use to support the care of this material? Because you are trying to create a relationship with the material, it can be helpful to use language that personifies the tools. Examples might include giving instructions such as "Give it a bath" to refer to rinsing the brush, talking about "good/bad hair days" when discussing care of bristles, or saying "as softly as petting a tiny mouse" when discussing how to get paint from the palette onto their brush.

- What steps will you include (consider setup, use of material, care of material, and cleanup)?

- Now try introducing watercolor in your setting.

Afterward, reflect: What went well? What challenges did you encounter? What might you do differently next time?

I encourage you to try the following materials exploration so that you can experience firsthand the relationship between big questions, materials, and thinking.

Materials Exploration: Materials as Tools for Thinking

This will help you explore the relationship between literacy, play, and the arts.

- **Provocation:** What is the relationship between literacy, play, and the arts?

- **Materials needed:** the loose parts you collected in small containers for collage, a twelve-by-eighteen-inch piece of paper or fabric to define your work area, and a journal and pen to capture your thinking

- **Prepare your environment:** See images throughout this book for ideas on organizing materials.

- **Getting started:** Set up your loose-parts collage collection in a quiet space. Spend some time playing around with these materials to develop your own theories about the relationships between literacy, play, and the arts.

    As you move the materials, pay attention to your own thinking. What do you already know about the relationship between literacy, play, and the arts? What questions come up for you? What surprises you? How do the materials offer new metaphors? What new ideas come up as you have a go at expressing your thinking through materials?

- **Reflect:** After you spend some time playing with materials, get out your journal and reflect through writing. What is the relationship between literacy, play, and the arts? What are the implications of this theory for your work with children in your classroom? What are you left wondering? How did using these materials as tools for thinking help you grow your theory in new ways?

Action Steps: Enrich Your Story Workshop Practice

🖋 If the problem of transmission is motivating to you, read Ursula Le Guin's essay "Telling Is Listening" (2004). Focus your observations on the patterns you notice in your own interactions with others. Keep a journal reflecting on these observations.

🖋 If you want to reflect some more on the power of children's ideas, watch Greta Thunberg's (2018) TEDxStockholm talk about her school strike for climate change. Listen to what she says about school. Reflect on the connections you make and the ways in which you might reconceptualize your classroom as a place where the change she seeks might become a reality. Consider the implications of story workshop on these possibilities.

🖋 If embracing uncertainty feels uncomfortable to you (like most people!), keep a journal about your experience with it. In what ways does it make you come alive? In what ways does it shut you down? Build a support system to lean on when you feel too far out of your comfort zone.

EDUCATOR INTERVIEW: TRUST THE PROCESS

Excerpted from an interview with Shelby Majure, kindergarten teacher KairosPDX, Portland, Oregon

KAIROSpdx is a public charter school in Portland, Oregon, serving children in grades K–5. KairosPDX is a nonprofit organization focused on delivering excellent, equitable education to underserved children, their families, and their communities. Our mission is to eliminate the prolific racial achievement and opportunity gaps by cultivating confident, creative, compassionate leaders who exceed expectations.

In one of the first story workshops I tried to facilitate, I asked the children what they wanted to learn about . . . and they were excited about outer space. So I tried to get clay and little astronaut figurines and I suggested to the children that we were going to pretend like we were blasting off to space. Then I asked them to tell a story about it. They were just acting out these space stories, and all of a sudden, they were like, "I have stories to tell."

That's what I loved about it. Story workshop allowed them to tell all of their imaginative and creative stories, without being worried that "I don't have the words to write this." Story workshop seemed to give them that connection. And it was that connection that . . . I don't know, can be really forced, and that's what I had been trying before—to just ask children to use sight words and write very simple sentences. But it squashed the imagination. These five- and six-year-olds have incredible imaginations and incredible stories to tell, but they don't always have the words to write them yet. And it just took off.

After I introduced clay, I introduced watercolors and then bookmaking. And slowly, it was like most of the kids were choosing watercolor and book-making. It was this slow progression from play to writing. Story workshop is this beautiful transition into writing. It eases the anxiety of the writing.

I think of one child in particular who came into kindergarten and he didn't know any of his letters, or any of his sounds, but he was so creative. He made really detailed drawings—detailed stories. He would tell me the stories, and they were super, super detailed. I remember the first time that he wrote letters down. He told me he wanted to write the words. *He* wanted to write them. It was like this internal motivation. For him, that I would try to read the drawing, wasn't exactly the story he was telling. He seemed to get to a point where he was determined to write on his own because he wanted to say what he was thinking. And by spring he was writing complete sentences.

I have children who write books and put them in our classroom library on their own. They write during choice time. They choose writing. So many of these children didn't know any letters or sounds when they arrived and story workshop offered this pivotal experience where they were supported to realize, "I want to tell my story, and so I'd better learn how to do it!"

My advice to other teachers who want to try story workshop would be to trust the process. It's messy, and it seems at first like maybe this isn't really writing. But those monumental moments really sold me because they convinced me it was working. Trust the process.

•••••••••••••••••••

"Stories are important because you can hear about someone else and you can learn about yourself."

—Ginger (age 9)

•••••••••••••••••••

CHAPTER FOUR

Invitation and Negotiation: Setting Expectations and Inviting Children to Create

During invitation and negotiation, the teacher gives a daily overview of the materials available and the teacher and students make agreements about where each child will get started and spend their time during story creation. Here's a sneak peek into invitation and negotiation:

Sarah: So if you are still on the rug, raise your hand if you know where you want to get started this morning. Think about what story you want to share this morning.

Asher: I want to go to small world this morning and make a story about when animals fall in love.

See page ix on how to access these videos.

Video 4.1 Invitation and Negotiation: Children Ages 5–7

Video 4.2 Invitation and Negotiation: Children Ages 3–5

Video 4.3 Invitation and Negotiation: Children Ages 6–8

Video 4.4 Negotiating the Need for New Paper: Children Ages 6–8

Sarah: Have you talked to Milo about his penguin story?

Asher: No . . .

Sarah: It seems like they are pretty connected! Milo, you have a story about penguins falling in love.

Asher: [Turning to Milo] You can help me! I'm making a story about a lot of animals falling in love.

You can see more in a video of this session (Video 4.1) and videos of several other classes (Videos 4.2 through 4.4).

What Is Invitation and Negotiation?

Invitation and negotiation is the part of story workshop that lies between provocation and story creation. It is time given to each individual, briefly, to voice plans, goals, and intentions for the work time that will follow and to negotiate agreement with the teacher on all of these things. Based on the relationship the teacher has with the child, the history of the child's work, and their shared intentions and expectations, the teacher has the opportunity to check in, listen, nudge, encourage, and hold accountable. As teachers encourage individual children to articulate their plan and the rest of the children listen, new ideas and words become a shared part of the culture that develops. Teachers make their expectations clear and structure routines that support one child, but that exchange has influence on the whole community.

Writing Workshop Connection: *Transitioning to Independent Work*

Writing workshop teachers develop a variety of structures and strategies to transition children between a minilesson and independent writing time. Sometimes children are dismissed in various ways to move into writing. Sometimes teachers require children to state an intention. Sometimes they ask children to name a way they expect to use the minilesson in their writing that day. Sometimes they ask children to say what they are planning to write about. Teachers in both writing workshop and story workshop take care to help children focus as they head to work.

Figure 4.1 Weekly Memory Keeping Form

WEEKLY MEMORY KEEPING FORM					
Name	Monday	Tuesday	Wednesday	Thursday	Friday

Teacher as Memory Keeper: Supporting Each Child to Get Where They Want to Go

Invitation and negotiation is a commitment to the particular and to the individual. This is where the child and their work and the teacher and their research meet up for a moment in genuine relationship and authentic inquiry. It is a moment of uncertainty that is rich in potential. If provocation is a game of toss with the group of children, invitation and negotiation is a moment to play with each child individually, knowing that they all like to engage in the game a little differently.

Teachers play an important role as memory keepers for the children from one day to the next. Using organizational tools such as the

Weekly Memory Keeping Form (Online Resource 4.1, shown here in Figure 4.1) teachers can, at a glance, remind a child what they were working on the previous session and help them productively move forward. Teachers can question children's intentions when they jump from one story to the next or when they seem unfocused. Teachers can gently challenge children to try something new and hold them accountable for the nudges they give. Children experience the close and careful attention of adult listeners who present themselves as an authentic audience who value their work deeply and who have high expectations for both their processes and their products.

Below are a few examples of the way teachers might use the Weekly Memory Keeping Form or freestyle journals to help them keep track of what students are working on.

> Beauty always takes place in the particular, and if there are no particulars, the chances of seeing it go down.
>
> —Elaine Scarry, *On Beauty and Being Just* (2011, 18)

Teachers take notes to help children remember what they are working on and to help them think about what might happen next.

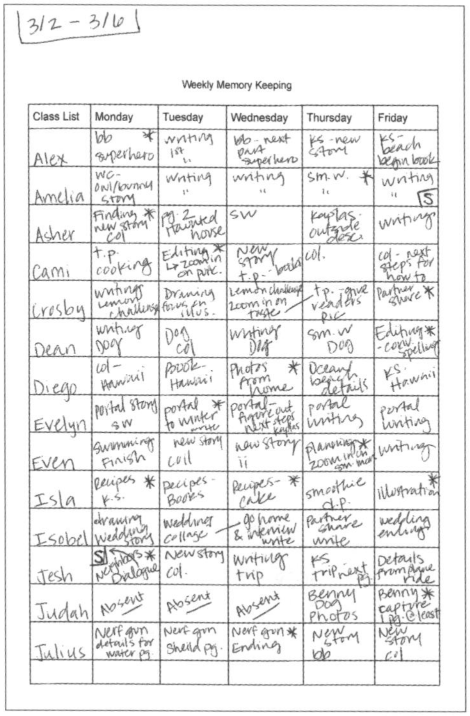

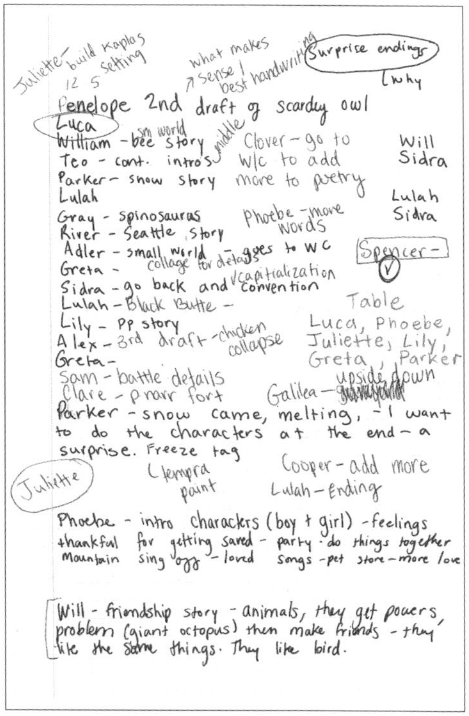

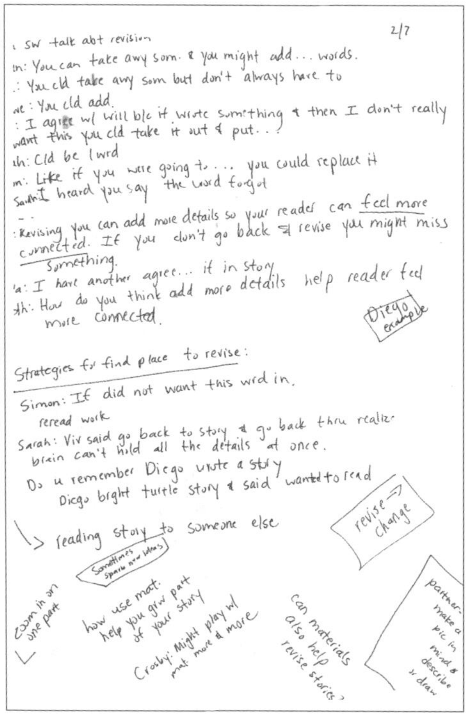

Weekly Memory Keeping

What Invitation and Negotiation Sounds Like

Teachers ask the following kinds of questions, and children respond with a plan as they transition to story creation:

- What's your plan? What are you working on?
- What material are you going to use? What tools do you need?
- Where will you find your story?
- Are you finding a new story or revisiting one?
- What part of your story are you working on?
- What's your intention? What material might help you with that? Why?
- You used blocks yesterday and got stuck. What new material might help you get unstuck today?
- How will you capture your story?
- What new material will you try? What might happen if you tell that story in a new material today?
- Yesterday you made a plan to _____. Is that still your plan?
- Please start by capturing what you found yesterday before you move to a new material to find out more.
- Would you like to start by telling a friend what you've got so far?
- How might you grow that idea? What will help you?
- How will you know if that material is supporting you or distracting you?
- What are you struggling with and how can I help you?
- What will you do if you get stuck?

Making Time for Everyone

In real life, working extensively with each individual every day isn't possible and it's not likely necessary. To keep invitation and negotiation focused on what is most important each day, teachers might try strategies such as these:

- Dismissing a group of children all at once: "If you are going back to writing today and you know which part you're going to start with, you can go get started."

- Checking in with individuals before story workshop begins, during cleanup, during individual conferences, or during story sharing the day before: "I already checked in with James, Aleysha, Ginger, and Chen, so you can go get started." Or "Ruby, you made a plan during sharing yesterday, so you can go get started."

- Calling on individual children to share plans and having them immediately get to work. This takes no more than a few seconds per child. If further negotiation is needed, children can get their work and then come back to the meeting area to check in after the rest have gotten started.

- Negotiating with individuals before story workshop begins: "Yesterday you got stuck, so what can we do to support you today?"

While it's important for children to hear one another's plans because it's an important strategy for setting expectations, developing a culture of story workshop, and growing shared language and understanding, it's not critical that every child hears every other child's plan every day. At times you'll want the whole group to stay for the entire sharing of plans. At other times, you'll want to send children off to story creation as they share their plans.

I hope that it's beginning to make sense that story workshop functions as a whole structure that is not especially reliant on sequence. In other words, if you would like to think more about this transition time between whole-group and independent work, you could start here. You can begin to construct your story workshop practice from anywhere within the structure and observe, reflect, and add on as it makes sense and works for you, the children and families you work with, and your school community.

When teachers take the time to get to know the interests of the children individually, they can better support them as they set intentions for their writing projects.

Nurturing Empathy and Solidarity Between Young Writers and Their Teachers

Story workshop supports teachers to create a classroom environment that welcomes, sustains, and interrogates the complexity of the relationship between words and ideas and emotions and experience so that complexity becomes an expected, celebrated norm. Ursula Le Guin writes: "Human communication cannot be reduced to information. The message not only involves, it is, a relationship between speaker and hearer. The medium in which the message is embedded is immensely complex, infinitely more than a code: it is a language, a function of a society, a culture, in which the language, the speaker, and the hearer are all embedded" (2004, 187). Each small moment of invitation and negotiation is embedded in this complexity.

Exchanges during invitation and negotiation require children to meet up with the authority that is the teacher. This is significant because it means that these small moments create repeated opportunity for us to be intentional about the experience with authority we want children to have. As the teacher, my focus may be on supporting the development of language and literacy skill, but the way I invite and negotiate expectations for the children's work can either reinforce the status quo relationship—including whatever kinds of implicit biases or culturally influenced assumptions might be in play—or challenge it. Teachers can be deliberate about what they give children an opportunity to practice—not only to craft strong leads or use correct punctuation but also to ask questions when something doesn't make sense, to defend an idea, to make productive choices, and to collaborate with both adults and peers. We don't need to work so hard to be objective. We can focus on the subject (the child)

Teachers frequently ask children if they'd like to tell them their story, and then they listen with genuine interest and curiosity.

and be curious about the intersubjectivity (the ecology) of the community both within and outside the classroom. We can regard each child with love, complicit in their search for meaning and relationship, willing to struggle and celebrate together with them (Rinaldi 2005). This kind of solidarity is what invites children to work *as themselves* toward goals that become shared as a result of meaningful negotiation.

The following story from the classroom reveals the possibility that exists when teachers and children negotiate during story workshop. While not all of the invitations and negotiations that take place between Kerry and Maxine in this story happened exclusively during invitation and negotiation (see again "Making Time for Everyone," on page 100), the spirit of the exchanges is representative of this important part of the story workshop structure each day.

Teachers can encourage children to see each other as resources and offer them practice with turning to one another for support.

Pictures of Practice
Helping Children Get Where They Want to Go Before They Know Where They're Going

Early one school year, a first grader named Maxine got excited about an idea. She and Kerry negotiated the use of watercolor paint over the next several days so she could explore images that would support her to grow her idea into a story. Maxine's eagerness to return to this story each day led Kerry to believe that she was very invested in it.

Later that week, Maxine decided she wanted to work with clay, and Kerry thought this was a fine idea because she knew that a new material would help Maxine grow her idea in new ways. Maxine was focused for a short time, but then her attention shifted to what other people were doing. She began to use her great sense of humor to stir up silliness throughout the classroom.

Kerry was curious about what had happened. Uncertainty set in and she wondered how she might nudge Maxine back toward focus. To be honest, her first impulse was to do more than nudge. It was to instruct Maxine to find a new story. But Kerry wanted Maxine to be in charge of her own work. She knew it wouldn't happen if she took control and told Maxine what to do. So instead of using her authority to direct her to "find a new story" or "make another choice," Kerry decided she would step back and invite her to try a new material.

During preparation the next day, Kerry made decisions to support this invitation. Kerry predicted that having the clay available in the room would make it difficult for Maxine to engage with another material. So she didn't offer it as a choice that day. This made invitation and negotiation with Maxine difficult. Maxine was not happy about the disappearance of the clay. She insisted that no other material would work for her and then dug her heels in and refused to budge.

Kerry was again tempted to instruct Maxine to find a new story, but amid this uncertainty, she managed to slow down and ask questions.

Kerry: Maxine, what is it about the clay that was feeling so helpful to you?

Maxine: The size. I can make a whole town with it.

[Maxine's response gave Kerry a window into her intent and needs, and she tried to build a bridge.]

Kerry: I wonder what other materials might support the same kind of inspiration that the clay provided. What about trying big blocks? They're big.

Maxine: There are never enough, and they will fall over. That will not work.

Kerry: What about painting on large paper at the easel?

Maxine: Nope! Not big enough and we might not even have the right colors I need.

[Kerry was as frustrated as Maxine was and she had to resist her impulse to take control of Maxine's experience. But she was convinced that Maxine cared about her idea and now she had a window into the affordances of the material Maxine was looking for. Maxine couldn't see beyond what she already knew. But Kerry could.]

Kerry: Hold on, I have an idea. I'll be right back.

Kerry ran into the back closet and brought out a very large piece of cardboard. Maxine brightened with fresh possibilities. Kerry had playfully offered Maxine a way out of her corner, and Maxine playfully accepted. (See Figures 4.2 and 4.3.)

Figures 4.2 and 4.3

Figure 4.4 "Christmastown"

Page 1: "Rrrrr!"

Page 2: "I rock!!!"

Soon, Maxine shared her writing with Kerry, and it was clear that the story wasn't over quite yet. She read each page of her book, titled "Christmastown." (See page 4.5.)

"Rrrr!" (See page 1.)

"I rock!!!" (See page 2.)

"Hohoho! Shut up!"

"Santa! Be nice!" (See page 3.)

"What the fet? Uh-oh!" (See page 4)

Kerry interrupted the story at this point and cautiously asked Maxine, "What does 'What the fet' mean?"

Maxine replied, "You know, like Boba Fett from Star Wars."

With noted skepticism, Kerry decided to accept this explanation, and Maxine finished reading.

"White out!!!" (See page 5.)

Kerry wanted to shout, "Maxine, what the Fett?!" This wasn't the kind of story Kerry knew Maxine was capable of writing, and after all that time invested, she didn't seem to care about it very much. Kerry tried to help Maxine figure out where things went wrong. She asked her many questions about the characters, the setting, the plot. And with frustration, Maxine replied, "I don't really know. I think that's what I'm trying to find out."

Ultimately, Kerry's effort was to find a way to connect with Maxine through a process of invitation and negotiation, in the most generous, compassionate, and authentic way she could. She wanted to preserve Maxine's humanity and retain her dignity. As I wrote in Chapter 1, on a perceptual level, school is indistinguishable from "real" life. These encounters between teacher and child create embodied reactions in both. They inform what can be imagined going forward. In an interview I once did with Karen Gallas, she told me:

> I see myself as part of the audience, as part of the community—
> I'm there, too—I get to say what I think. And I usually find
> that when I am having a visceral response as an audience
> member, that's when my response is most effective. Instead
> of saying, "Don't do that here. It's wrong," I'd rather say,
> "That makes me so uncomfortable and I don't like it because
> it scares me," or whatever. That's the way I see my responses

as authentic response, rather than "let's quash the response."
So, yes, I do intervene in that way now, but I've found through
my latest work that I have to do it as a full member, not as
the member with the shove who's going to push it. Children
have taught me to do that. . . . The children see that as an
appropriate response when you are truly honest about things.
(MacKay 2002, 145)

Kerry could have pushed the shove that she had in her pocket because
she was the teacher. But Maxine was just as frustrated as she was. Kerry was
considerate of Maxine's perceptual, embodied experience and the impact it
would have on her future predictions about her abilities as a young writer in
school. So Kerry invited Maxine to return to materials even though she wasn't
feeling confident—even though she was concerned that Maxine was wasting
time and she was concerned that she herself was doing something wrong.

Maxine worked with a loose-parts collection that had been curated to
provide a wintery theme. Kerry *forced* herself to bite her tongue, withhold
judgment, stay in inquiry, and allow just a little more time (even though
none of this was in her comfort zone). She watched and waited and tried to
facilitate Maxine's process rather than push Maxine to satisfy the teacher's
authority.

And it wasn't long before Kerry heard Maxine say, "Kerry! I found my
story! I'm going to give Rudolph a voice!" She sat down and began her second draft. And Kerry saw a level of engagement that she hadn't ever seen
in Maxine before.

Here is her story: (Figure 4.5 is a sample of what this story looked like:
written text poured on every page.)

> It all started somewhere in Christmas Town . . . where there
> is a castle and Santa Claus!!! No flowers grow. "Rudolph the
> red-nosed reindeer," all the other reindeer jeered.
>
> "Why are you teasing me?" Rudolph said.
> "Because you have a red nose," they said.
> "But I am like you," said Rudolph.

Page 3 "Hohoho! Shut up!"
"Santa! Be nice!"

Page 4 "What the fet? Uh-oh!"

Page 5 "White out!!!"

"No, you are *not* like us," they said, "because you have a red nose!"

"So?" said Rudolph.

"So? Ha!" they said.

"The only difference is that I have a red nose," said Rudolph.

"Exactly!" they said.

Then, Santa walked over and said, "What is going on?" They said, "He . . ."

Rudolph interrupted, "They are teasing me!"

"What?" they said. "We didn't . . ."

"I believe Rudolph," said Santa. "But it is time to hop on the sleigh. Run!"

The reindeer ran toward the sleigh. The reindeer had to be quick. When the elves hitched them up and Santa was in the sleigh, they were off! Delivering presents to the boys and girls of the world.

Maxine reads *Christmas Town* to her class.

Figure 4.5

Reflection

- How would you describe this process of invitation and negotiation between Kerry and Maxine?
- How did having access to materials allow Kerry to support Maxine as a writer and help them stay in dialogue with each other?
- What kind of assumptions did Kerry seem to struggle with? How do you speculate that her work with Maxine supported her to reframe those assumptions?
- How would you describe Maxine's experience with Kerry's authority?
- What associations do you imagine Maxine makes between school and the writing she is expected to do there?
- When you look back at your three dispositions of citizen worldmakers, how do they find their place within these reflections?

Staying Grounded: Nudging Children Out of Their Comfort Zones

Children expect from adults the capacity to help them navigate the hard stuff—the risk and change that learning requires—so they can experience the joy of having done so and so they can learn that joy lives alongside struggle. Sometimes that means that teachers have to nudge children out of their comfort zones. Teachers can hold a vision of possibility for children they can't yet imagine for themselves, like Kerry did for Maxine. Kerry could imagine Maxine's potential even when Maxine could not—and even though Kerry didn't know for sure how they would get there.

Sometimes children aren't very cooperative negotiators, and they don't see immediate possibility in the invitations they receive. Uncertainty can come on fast in those moments for everyone, and it helps to have thought ahead of time about how you will handle it. Maybe they've decided to abandon a story that seemed so promising the day before. Maybe they want to play with blocks for what feels like one hour too many. Maybe they want to write when it seems like they could benefit from more time with materials. Maybe they want to work with a friend and you're skeptical that it will be productive. Maybe they've been working in dramatic play all week and you aren't seeing any story take form. Our response to these common challenges is informed by our beliefs and values. This is the heart of the distinction between scripted and programmatic instruction and instruction that is developed based on a teacher's own experience, intellect, and creativity—and their willingness to not push their shove. If entering into an exchange of this sort, with this degree of uncertainty, sounds risky to you, consider the following thoughts from Tom Newkirk:

> **Even in established medical practice, with a research base far more solid than anything in education, physicians are constantly experimenting, as each patient differs in tolerance for particular medicines, and even in willingness to take them. . . . We actually are suspicious of physicians who seem to be just following protocol, who seem on automatic pilot. And I would also suspect that as teachers, we are at our *best* when we are "experimenting" with children (and ourselves). If I am trying something new,**

there is a sense of anxious expectation; I pay attention to what happens, assess, and modify. I feel most alive, engaged when I am doing something new. If, in the name of certainty, this privilege to experiment is stripped away, we will all be the losers for it. (2014, 221)

Our goal is to pay attention to the children every day—each of them unique—to assess and to modify the environment, the experience, the questions, and the expectations in a way that makes them feel most alive and engaged in their work. When the teacher enters the relationship that way, they give the children an experience with a culture and society in which they and their stories matter. Teachers can harness the privilege to experiment and put it in service of changing the persistent assumptions the world outside the classroom tends to hold about teaching, learning, school, children, and childhood.

What *do* you believe about children? What do you believe about the mistakes they make? What do you believe about children and writing? What you believe matters. Your beliefs frame your attention, they inform your assumptions, and they predict your behavior. The more aware you are of your beliefs *and* of how your beliefs inform your action, the more possibility you have to change the things you'd like to change.

Try This: *Connecting Our Beliefs with Our Intentions*

During invitation and negotiation, children and teachers set intentions, try things out, reflect on what happened, and then make adjustments. Again and again.

Begin by setting an intention or goal for yourself. Be your own memory keeper by writing your intention down in a journal or notebook. This can be an intention for your teaching or for your personal life. It can be something in the distant future or something you want to make happen today, no matter how big or small.

Consider the extent to which the following factors influence your intention:

- prior experience

- hopes and dreams

- geography, location, place

- values, culture, religion

- early life and education

- professional desires, ambitions, or failures

- likes or dislikes

- financial experience or outlook

- politics

- physical or health history

- current mood and energy level

- books, television, websites

- something you were told by someone you admire

What do you discover about your intention when you look at it through these various lenses? As you consider these many influences, what surprises you? How does being aware of your influences give you more awareness of your intentions? How might a practice of framing your intentions in a variety of personal ways support you to be a better negotiator with children as you invite them to frame theirs?

Keeping the Head and the Heart Connected

Story gives our internal experiences external form. It is a weaving of what we feel, what we think, and what we imagine. The first three elements of the story workshop structure are opportunities to create a lived experience for teachers and children to navigate together with their whole selves in order to strengthen each person's ability to invent, develop, and share their stories. Preparation, provocation, and invitation and negotiation help teachers create structure in order to enter into a process alongside children that is inherently individual and uncertain and that is filled with emotion.

In spite of how much we know about the interconnectedness of cognition and emotion, we rarely make adequate space to acknowledge and work with these realities in ways that would benefit us all. We still try to control emotion—to anesthetize it—in order to make children more compliant with instructional procedures. Invitation and negotiation offers a daily opportunity to put a check on the experience with authority we are providing to each child. We need to practice observing ourselves in those interactions. Though we always want what's best for the children, it remains countercultural for us to recognize, as a first priority, the humanity in every child we have the privilege to work alongside. In her book *All About Love*, bell hooks writes, "There can be no love without justice. Until we live in a culture that not only respects but also upholds basic civil rights for children, most children will not know love" (2018, 19-20). Upholding basic civil and human rights in our classrooms is within our control as the adults in those classrooms. But we must first become able to articulate our own image of children, childhood, and learning, as well as our belief about what school is for, and we must connect the dots between what happens in school and what happens in the world. This effort can be supported in the same way story workshop supports children to find and share their stories: by using materials to explore and reflect on our own experience of embodied learning.

Materials Exploration: Bringing a Story to Materials

🖋 **Getting started:** Start by choosing a story. Maybe this is a story you have already started writing or maybe it's one that you'd like to tell. It can be real or imaginary, something you are planning on sharing or a reflection you plan to keep to yourself. Either way, choose something you care about and want to put some time into.

🖋 **Materials needed:** It's up to you this time. Consider what material you think might help you bring a part of your story to life. For example, loose-parts collage offers a great deal of flexibility. The materials are fluid and have the ability to move and change without leaving a permanent mark. Black pen, on the other hand, leaves a mark that cannot be removed. There is value to both of these experiences with materials; each has the potential to inspire different kinds of connections and metaphors and to leave you with an experience that deepens your reflection.

🖋 **Prepare the environment:** Set up the material and space with an attention to care and allow yourself to use that material to tell a part of your story.

🖋 **Reflect:** What happened when you took your story to the material? In what ways did your story grow or change? What new thinking came up as you used this material? What surprised you? What challenged you? What would you do differently next time?

Action Steps: Enrich Your Story Workshop Practice

- If the issue of civil and human rights inspires you, familiarize yourself with the United Nations Declaration of the Rights of the Child. Contemplate the possible reasons why the United States remains the only United Nations member country that has not ratified the declaration. What are the cultural and societal implications for children living in this country, especially when you consider bell hooks' assertion that there can be no love without justice? What is the role of schools? What role can you play?

- If offering children more power to make choices about their work in the classroom feels like too big a stretch all at once, find a small time of day or a project of limited duration in which you can experiment and reflect on what happens.

- If you are uncertain about how well you know each of the children you work with, list their names from memory and make a list of everything you know about them personally. Try to focus on the personal rather than the academic. If there are children whom you know less well than others, focus on getting to know them better and see what happens!

EDUCATOR INTERVIEW: AN EXPERIENCE OF FREEDOM

Excerpted from an interview with Aeriale Johnson, second-grade teacher Washington Elementary School, San Jose, California

I HAVE A WRITING WORKSHOP BACKGROUND AND I HAVE BEEN attending institutes at the Teachers College Reading and Writing project for the past ten years. Prior to that I'd read Donald Graves and a lot of the writing workshop pioneer researchers. I'm kind of a junkie that way. I've been teaching for many years, but the past two have been at Washington Elementary School in San Jose, California. Our population is about 91 percent English language learners.

It's safe to say that from the government's perspective, these kids are low-performing. Of course I don't believe that or agree with it at all. I know that the disparity between what's expected of them and their "performance" has everything to do with instructional practices and not the capacity of the children. This year I work with second grade and I have thirty students in my class, which is a whole, whole lot. When we started this school year, twenty-two of them were either in intervention or had an IEP.

I believe that all children need to play. All children can create art and interact with materials. Having access to these languages is incredibly powerful for English language learners to be able to process and figure out what it is they're trying to say. When we expect children to sit down and start writing in English when they barely speak it, we do a tremendous disservice to them.

I think that the children who haven't played a lot need to do that. That's the first thing. When you have the expectation that they are going to write, they're going to eventually rise to meet that, and they see their peers, the other students in the class, who are writing at the end of the workshop when it's sharing time. Their friends share and the children who may not be writing so much yet think, "I want to do that!" Kids want to do right. They do. So just give them space and time and really pay attention to what they're doing and why they're doing it.

The other day a child who has some fear, articulation issues, severe language issues, and who is a language learner on top of all that was painting and he told this incredible story. It was the most words we have heard him speak this entire school year. It was so beautiful. I'm convinced he never would have said any of that had it not been for an environment that invited him to use materials and to play with language. In my context, materials and time to play seem to offer an opportunity for kids to process the trauma they've experienced. My kids have a lot of it, unfortunately. I think an environment organized this way gives them an opportunity to process their experience in a place that is safe and nonjudgmental. They may not have the words to express all of that trauma, but they can certainly express it through color and textures and play.

Story workshop taps into the natural creativity that exists within all children so that they can speak and ultimately write successfully without an adult telling them what to do. A sentence frame tells children, "I decided what language you need, and this is how you need to say it." Materials say, "Oh, I see what you're doing here. Here are the words to describe that." It's a totally different thing.

I worry about what happens next for these children, where freedom is not a mindset for learning that all of their teachers will value. It helps me to keep in mind something that Carla Shalaby, author of the important book *Troublemakers*, once told me. She said, "Aeriale, you can't set them free. That's not your job. You can only give them the opportunity to experience freedom. And I don't think that they are ever going to forget that." Story workshop helps me give them that experience. And no, I don't think they'll forget it. Once we've experienced freedom, none of us ever do.

"Words have superpowers because
they make people feel things!"

—Will (age 6)

CHAPTER FIVE
Story Creation

During story creation, children play with materials, talk to each other, and tell and write stories. Teachers work with small groups and individuals, supporting their creative process, their access to materials, their social exchanges, and their growing academic proficiency.

Here is a snippet of what happened when Kerry sat down to check in with a group of children who were playing with kinetic sand in small, individual trays:

Kerry: So what's your story going to be?

Millie: How to make this giant cake!

Kerry: How to make a cake?

Millie: Yeah, but you can't eat it.

Kerry: What do you do with a cake you can't eat?

Millie: Ah . . . well, it's supposed to be for bugs. It's a bug cake.

Kerry: Oh, it's a bug cake. So you can't eat it but somebody can?

Millie: Yeah, a bug.

Video 5.1 Story Creation: Children Ages 5–7

Video 5.2 Kerry and Mead (Age 7) Confer

Video 5.3 Creating Stories with Loose Parts: Children Ages 3–5

Video 5.4 Everybody Sing: Children Ages 3–5

Video 5.5 Owen Translates His Story: Children Ages 3–5

Video 5.6 Creating Recipes: Children Ages 3–5

See page ix on how to access these videos.

Kerry: A bug can.

Evelyn: What does it have in it?

Millie: Well, it has . . .

Evelyn: Some bugs like eating dung.

Watch Video 5.1 to hear Kerry reflect on this session of story creation as well as to see what happened as these children continued their discussion. In the online resources, you will find a variety of additional videos offering windows into story creation and the role teachers play during this time. (Videos 5.2 through 5.6.)

What Is Story Creation? Exploring the World in Every Word—or Not

Story creation is an independent work time that makes up the bulk of a session of story workshop. It usually lasts between forty and fifty minutes, but it's OK to start with less if that's all you have. It is a time devoted to making words come alive with personal knowing and perspective and conceptual understanding in order for authors to be able to construct and share meaning—to make sense of their relationship to the world through story.

Pictures of Practice
What Stories Live Inside Pink?

Some three- to five-year-old children were having a small-group discussion:

Alden: Pink makes you have love because it's the color of your heart.

Emory: That light pink reminds me of the color of my house.

Montgomery: When I see pink I really like the color dark pink. It reminds me of butterflies that are in the shade.

Sanjay: It reminds me of my sister because she likes pink so, so much. So many things in her room are pink—her walls, her Christmas wrapping paper, two bunnies, and her strawberry house. I like bright pink and dark pink and spooky pink.

Bishop: My daddy's favorite color is pink because it was his favorite as a little kid.

Sanjay: Our brain is pinkish-red. And worms too.

Emory: The dawning sunset.

Montgomery: Pigs. Gum.

Sanjay: Balloons. Cotton candy. My heart is a reddish pink.

Alden: I'm making my brain. It has these tiny things that help you remind yourself. This is the memory's collector [dark pink]. Light pink is ear tubes.

Sanjay: When my mom leaves, my brain cuts apart.

The children begin to work with materials and tell stories. Here are two of them:

> **Sanjay:** These are love barnacles in your heart. They're really thick because they're different from ocean barnacles. My heart is connected to my brain. They grow inside when you get to know someone that you really love. The empty white spaces are the spaces for memories.

> **Bishop:** This is my brain and heart. They made friends a long time ago when we was babies. The heart was six to ten years old and the brain was six. The brain moved away from his old house and moved with his family to a new house. Then a new friend came over to the friend brain's old house. The heart mom and kid made pineapple carrot muffins in the morning. The next morning he had a playdate with his friend Brain at the heart's house. Then when the brain's mom dropped the brain off at the heart's house, they ate the muffins all together. Then the next night the brain slept over at the heart's house and they got to paint their nails.

Did you ever imagine that so many stories lived inside the word *pink*? So many different sensory images and memories and concepts and varied ways of knowing? Many different worlds live inside every word. Words can be full of active imagery and perceptual memory and cultural significance, but depending on the quality of the conceptual and perceptual world held within them, they can as easily be a collection of letters and sounds meaning nothing much. What we say has no inherent meaning of its own. Pink doesn't just mean pink. Red may not mean the same red in your head and mine. You may have noticed, as you read the discussion before the stories, how much the children relied on each other's ideas—how they picked them up and used them as though they were another loose part to play with. As children practice seeing each other as resources, they experience the myriad things they each know as vital to their own ability to perceive new possibility. In this chapter, we'll explore the role of play and the arts in supporting a recognition of, a curiosity for, and a value in difference, diversity, and collaboration.

Writing Workshop Connection: *Independent Writing*

Like story workshop, a session of writing workshop includes an extended period of time for independent work. During this time in writing workshop, children take their pieces through the writing process: prewriting, drafting, revising, editing, and publishing. Teachers confer with individuals and small groups to set goals, offer feedback, and make suggestions based on each individual's particular needs.

Writing workshop in the early years is guided by a belief in the capacity of very young children to pay attention to, wonder about, and make decisions about their craft and composition as writers. In both story workshop and writing workshop, teachers use children's own writing to teach writing skills and strategies. Children are often invited to write like readers and read like writers. There is a high value placed on the relationship between emergent reading and writing and an understanding that children gain important skills as early readers through writing and the opportunity it creates to read their own words.

Time to Create Stories

During story creation, children use art media to spark and explore ideas, but the goal is not for children to become skilled painters or sculptors. The goal is for teachers to create conditions that promote relaxed alertness, which nurtures capable, confident, engaged, and proficient writers in order to strengthen agency, empathy, identity, and meaning.

Human beings use symbols of many kinds to give shape to experience and invent a relationship to the rest of the world (Dyson 1990). Story creation happens within an environment that has been intentionally designed to turn up the

volume on perceptual experience because we know that there is a fundamental relationship between experience as we perceive it and symbol making, including, but not limited to, words. Beau Lotto writes, "Perception is not an isolated operation in our brains, but part of an ongoing process inside an *ecology*, by which I mean the relation of things to the things around them, and how they influence each other" (2017, 7). Every waking moment, we encounter the complexity of this ecology we are part of, and story is the way we navigate our way through it, making the worlds we live in as we go along.

Story creation is dedicated time for exploring the patterns and connections and relationships within this complex ecology using materials and processes of the arts through play. The truth is, we rely way too much on words to support children to learn how to use them. We know that children will play with pretty much anything they can get their hands on. And we know if they get their hands on something, they've got their minds on something. And once something is on our minds, we've got a story to tell. The words will come when children see them as useful tools to shape their inner experience into outer form and share it with others. Children will reveal the profound ideas they have about their experiences with the world. Take it from Milo, age six: "People maybe have a plan for what the future could be like, but then when someone else shows up and says, 'I want this to be a more wonderful place,' and they work a lot and really hard, it can be more wonderful than they even imagined at the beginning."

Words Create Worlds

In her book *Mind in Motion*, psychologist Barbara Tversky writes: "When thought overflows the mind, the mind puts it into the world" (2019, 190). The images and ideas attached to words—the stories that children tell—are put into the world as they overflow from within the child, who is continually trying to make meaning. The use of materials and time to play in story workshop drives the need for words by encouraging thoughts to overflow.

Not only do words contain the worlds that inspired their use, but they create worlds, too. According to neuroscientist Lisa Barrett, "predictions are primal" (2017b). What we already know seeds what we will continue to experience. A child may be in the most beautiful classroom in the world, surrounded by materials of the highest quality. But if, when the teacher says *writing*, the world the child imagines inside the word *writing* is one that is filled with emotion associated with boredom or failure, the child's perception of the classroom will be influenced by predictions of further boredom and humiliation. The concepts that inhabit the words you know drive the predictions you make about what will happen next, and those predictions are always intertwined with emotion. Beau Lotto writes, "Our sense of self, our most essential way of understanding existence, begins and ends with perception" (2017, 3). That is because "feeling comes first" (Tversky 2019, 42). At lightning speed, your brain processes sensory input and makes predictions about what to pay attention to and what will happen next *before* thought ever becomes words or words become understanding. Materials and time to play help us slow that process down so that we have a chance to reflect on the world our words create and to make sure it's the one we want to live in. We learn that we can write new stories, as the child did with the blocks in Chapter 1. Elliot Eisner writes, "One of the large lessons the arts teach is how to secure the feelingful experience that slowed perception makes possible; the arts help students learn how to savor qualities by taking the time to really look so that they can see" (2002, 24). In the following story, the experience of Sam and Will help us see this possibility in action.

Pictures of Practice
Making a Chance to Connect

Six-year-old Sam was passionate about dinosaurs. Early in the school year he created many books full of beautiful and detailed illustrations of dinosaurs. He didn't quite yet see himself as a writer capable of scribing all the information he knew, but he eagerly made page after page of detailed drawings. Kerry began to look for ways to support Sam in having a go at writing words. She started to wonder what kinds of constraints she could impose to encourage him to take a risk without taking away his ability to make choices.

Several weeks into the school year, Kerry asked the children to choose something from the *currently living* natural world that they wanted to get to know better as they began research for a writing project. As Kerry predicted, Sam was not excited about this. He asked if he could please choose a dinosaur. But this project held the boundary Kerry created to challenge Sam, so she said that though he could not work with a dinosaur this time, he could choose anything else from this vast category. Sam stayed just within that boundary by choosing to study an alligator snapping turtle. Perhaps to his surprise, he seemed to enjoy the process of gathering information to share with others—a surprise that constraints on his choices helped him find.

One day Kerry asked the children to join a partner and allow their characters to "meet and get to know one another better." Sam (the alligator snapping turtle) and Will (the screech owl) became partners. Now, Sam and Will (the humans) were about as likely to be found playing together as an alligator snapping turtle and a screech owl. Sam said, "But we don't have anything in common." It was hard for them to make a decision about how to get started together. Will wanted to go to clay and Sam wanted to do *anything* else.

Sam and Will negotiate.

A word like *partner* seemed to hold images for Sam and Will that caused them to predict that their experience wouldn't go well. That prediction created anxiety and made it difficult for them to get started. The stories they were telling about each other, based on past experiences, led them to make predictions that sustained that story and the feelings that story created within and between them.

The boundary and expectation that they would do the work together led them, eventually, to choose to draw together. They drew a giant world, where the two of them lived together, and developed a story about how these two unlikely animals became friends. They, quite literally, drew a new world inside the word *partner*—one in which the two of them were friends. And a new story emerged full of new concepts, new possibilities, and new emotions.

They reflected on their experience later that day:

Sam: My partner is a screech owl and we're friends.

Will: We care about each other.

Sam: I wondered what a screech owl might be like at first.

Will: Both our animals were curious about each other.

Sam: At first I thought a screech owl might screech a lot so I didn't want to connect.

Will: And I thought snapping turtles couldn't swim and I was too shy to connect.

Kerry: So, what helped you to build your friendship with each other?

Sam: We sort of sorted out ideas about each other in our storage mind. And then we went into it with an open mind.

Will: And I was shy but I just tried to have a go!

Kerry: Do you think this might apply to how humans grow connections with each other, too?

Sam: Well, even if humans are kind of different, they're kind of the same, too. So, if you're a person and you get stuck just thinking someone else is too different from you, then you miss your chance to connect.

Kerry chose to prioritize the relationship between the children first because that held the meaning. She wanted them to strengthen their awareness of having moved beyond the rigid assumptions they had through

uncertainty and discomfort to a new way of seeing things. Their imaginations had expanded and Kerry wanted to focus on that critical process in order to strengthen their courage in the value of that process. According to Dr. Jennifer Eberhardt (2020), it is a reliance on rigid categories that creates and perpetuates bias. It takes practice to reimagine the worlds in the words that we use to name the concepts we understand so that we don't develop a belief that any one world is more right than another.

The world isn't fixed in that way, so our beliefs needn't be, either. And so that is the practice Kerry focused on first. The story and the writing came next. And, not incidentally, so did the words.

I see that screech owl. I do not know if I should d, do it. I, I, I, I, I, I will do it. . . . I want to make friends with the screech owl.

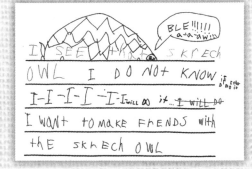

I was a war turtle. I would kill others. I also do everything bad!!! Don don don!!!

I needed to improve my tech. I did not have a clue how to! The screech owl?

I'll just have a go! Oh, I am not doing it. OK, I will do it!!!!!

That whole friend thing is kind of weird. Weeeelllllllllllll, ya!

that HOL FREN D thing is a kind uv WERD weeeeelll LLLLLL LLLLLLLLLL LLLLLLLLLLL LLLLL LLLLLL LL ya!

5

Still this whole friend thing is weird, but I really need better tech . . . so I just have a go. I jump on his head.

YES!

aa Hoo

STIL this hole FREND thing is WERD BUT I rily NEDE BETER tek... SO I GEST HAV A GO I GUMP ON HIS HEAD

6

Then I say sorry and he replies it's OK . . . I have another go!!! I do not injure him . . . But he said, "If you promise to . . ." "Yes, yes, yes, I will not throw you . . ." "I know—I know—I know."

O NO!

aa H!

then I say SORY and Hoe riPLISE it's OKAY I HAV A NUTHER GO !!! I DONOT INGER HIM...BUT HE SED "IF YOU PHOMIS TO..." "YES-YES I WILL not throw you!!!—I KNOW—I KNOW-I Know"

Wow! Friendship is good! I am going to keep this friendship forever!!!!!

WOW!

Frenrship is GOOD I am GOYNTO kepe this FRENDSHIP FONR EVEr!!!!!!!!!....

And it really did improve my tech. I use it for the better . . . oh and that screech owl is really smart. . . . We build homes for us and others instead of killing others.

aaND it rily did iproov MY tek I rous it FOn theBETER... ohaND that SKreych OWL is rily smart.... WE BILD HOMES FOR us and OTHERS insted uv killing others

The end

THE END

The constraint that Kerry put on Sam's choices created a context in which he had to navigate something new and somewhat uncomfortable. The context—the ecology—is what gave particular meaning to the words. Attending to the process within that ecology allowed the children to reconceptualize, reimagine, and reconstruct the world that lived inside the experience of *partner*, *friend*, and even *writing*. What children perceive through experience today will influence the predictions they make tomorrow (Barrett 2016). Lotto's words bear repeating: "Our sense of self . . . begins and ends with perception," (2017, 3).

We can help ourselves develop curiosity about difference by making an effort to habitually assume that no one ever sees the world the same way we do, even if they are right there next to you. We can't control what anyone else perceives, not even children. We can be intentional as we create the conditions in which children *will* perceive, and we can prepare ourselves to listen to and observe the ways they respond. It's not that children don't all learn in the same way; it's that not a single one of them sees the world in the same way that the teacher does or that any of their peers do. When we model a way to navigate that truth, we increase the likelihood that the children will, too. An equitable approach begins when the teacher understands that none of the children will perceive what they are trying to teach in the same way—and

the teacher doesn't expect them to. While teaching can be limited to the direct, planned interactions between student and teacher, learning never is. Debates over whether or not children all learn the same way are pointless unless we first consider the extent to which perception supports or interferes with what is being taught and understand that teachers cannot control that. We can only work to allow this insight to influence our own perception of the work—and then keep on doing that, as long as we work with children.

Try This: *Tappers and Listeners*

In their book *Made to Stick*, Dan and Chip Heath (2007) write about research done by a Stanford PhD student named Elizabeth Newton, who wrote a whole dissertation on what she called "tappers" and "listeners." Her study asked "tappers" to pick from a list of twenty-five well-known songs, like "Twinkle, Twinkle, Little Star," and tap out the rhythm on a table while another person acted in the role of "listener." The listener was supposed to guess the song based on the tapping. It turned out that listeners were only able to guess 2.5 percent of the songs. But what was really interesting was that the tappers, who were asked to guess the odds the listener would figure out the song correctly, predicted it would work 50 percent of the time. They thought their message would come across one out of two times.

Find a partner and give it a try! Think of a song you are sure you both know, such as "Happy Birthday" or "Single Ladies," and tap it for your listener. Reverse roles!

When the melody is so clear in your own mind, how hard is it to imagine the listener's perspective? As a listener, how difficult is it to imagine what the tapper is hearing in their mind? How do you relate these difficulties to the complexities of teaching and learning?

Materials Exploration: Using Materials to Translate Ideas

Words, like taps, are symbols for the tune you hear in your head. The melody carries the meaning. Eleven-year-old Nisa explains a strategy that has helped her bring a clearer melody to the words she uses when she hopes to share her ideas with others:

> One of the big parts of growing an idea is putting it into a new language in art or words. It's like translating. It's a really important part because if you can't do that nobody else can share the amazingness of your idea. Translating ideas helps other people to understand your ideas better. As you change your idea into something you can say or see that other people can understand, then you sort of understand it better yourself. It's a way of understanding not just for other people, but for yourself. You can think you understand something but when you translate it into another language, you really understand it more; what it is, compared to what you initially thought it was, is so different.

✐ **Materials needed:** Choose two materials that have different qualities, such as paint and small blocks. Grab your journal and something to write with. The purpose of this experience is to pay attention to what happens to your idea when you translate it between materials and between materials and words.

✐ **Getting started:** Use the materials you prepared to explore an idea you've been thinking about. You might start by asking yourself, "What is something that's been on my mind that feels important?" This could be a story you want to tell, a theory you have about something that's been happening in the classroom, in the world, or at home, or a challenge you've been experiencing. Spend at least fifteen minutes using the materials to explore this idea. Pay attention to what happens to your idea as you work to represent it in a material. After exploring this idea in this material, spend at least ten minutes writing down your current thinking in your journal.

🖋 **Prepare your second material:** When you finish writing, gather what you need to work with your next material. This could be right away or during your next available work session.

Use these new materials to explore the same idea that you began exploring before. Spend at least fifteen minutes using these new materials to continue exploring this idea. After exploring this idea with these materials, spend another ten minutes writing. Be sure to capture any new language, thoughts, feelings, or theories that came up after another experience with materials.

🖋 **Reflect:** Think back on your experience with these two different materials. Also, go back and reread your writing. What happened when you took an idea to materials? How did your language grow and change? What metaphors came up for you? What emotions came up? What did you notice about how your idea shifted, changed, or grew? How do you relate your experience to what Nisa describes?

The Power of the Arts

When children use the materials of the arts to explore the "amazingness" of their ideas in a variety of forms, they practice what it means to make meaning and to understand. Meaningful writing—writing that is constructed from experience and has the power to transform the experience of someone else—doesn't come from disembodied tapping. In another way to discuss Tversky's assertion about how thought overflows the mind, Elliot Eisner writes, "The writer starts the process of writing by seeing and by having an emotional response that is then transformed into words intended to capture the flavor of that response" (2002, 88). Words reach toward a listener or a reader, who translates them and transforms them into connections they find within their own ecology of experience. Theater critic Kenneth Lonergan (2003) writes, "I think we live so much in our imaginations—not just artist types but everyone—that in some ways the imaginative connection you get between a play or movie or book or painting or piece of music and its respective audience is as close as we ever get to each other." As Nisa explains, materials are tools of the imagination that bring us closer to our own ideas in order to share them through words that bring us closer to others. When children use materials, not only does it make it easier for other people to see what they mean, it makes it easier for them to see their own ideas.

It is critical for teachers of writing to remember that children don't make stories so they can learn how to write. They learn how to write so they can tell stories. And as we saw with Sam and Will, the context that forces the story to overflow from the mind is where the story really begins. "To begin a story is to make a choice from an infinity of possibilities, selecting one set rather than another. That is why it is not just fiction which is an exercise of the imagination, it is any construction of narrative coherence" (Rosen, paraphrasing Umberto Eco, 1986, 231). To select and organize coherence from such vast possibility, regardless of topic or genre, is a profoundly creative process that reveals the genius human beings are all capable of. But capacity doesn't become ability without an environment in which it can practice (Eisner 2002). If we can maintain a sense of awe and wonder at the process as we meet up with children who are creating stories, even when we don't yet understand what they're trying to

say, we'll be better equipped to support children to stay in charge of their own intention (Dyson 1990). When children's bodies are active within the context that fills words with their particular meaning, they are more likely to craft writing using words that are attached to a melody others can hear. Or at least, they are more likely to be *attuned* to whether others can hear the song because they are more likely to *care* that they do.

As we saw with Sam and Will, or with Paul in the first chapter, or with Maxine, use of the arts and the artful use of words help us learn to believe that difference is not deficiency. An equitable experience both in and out of the classroom fully relies on the promise of this concept taking hold. Maxine Greene writes of the arts as a critical tool to help us "overcome the inability to see others" (1995, 136). She goes on to say, "We are fully present to art when we understand what is there to be noticed in the world at hand, release our imaginations to create orders in the field of what is perceived, and allow our feelings to inform and illuminate what is there to be realized" (138). Imagination creates the possible, which is a prerequisite for perceiving what could be actual.

Only when we can perceive the actual in new ways do we acquire the potential to do things differently (Bruner 1986; Eisner 2002; Barrett 2017b). Ample use of the arts helps us all learn to believe that "normal" or "standard"—at least when it comes to human experience—is a fiction (Souto-Manning and Martell 2016). Through these processes, with materials in hand, children grow the courage they need to see the world through their own eyes and to tell their own truths for others to hear. The arts support us to stop looking for someone else to tell us we're right and stay focused on what *feels* right so we can share and seek connections and negotiate belonging.

Supporting Children During Story Creation

The teacher has a critical role in supporting children through story creation. Here are some things a teacher might consider as they work alongside children who are creating stories:

- What is the child's intention? What is the child trying to do?

- What materials might support that intention?

If the child is struggling, return to these questions until they find a story they care about. When the child is ready to tell a story, consider these questions:

- What story does the child tell?

- How can you respond to the story as a genuine audience with genuine emotion?

When talking with children about their stories, use supportive language like this:

- Can you tell me more about . . .

- I notice . . .

- That reminds me of . . .

- Your story makes me feel . . .

- I wonder . . . (where that idea came from/what will happen next/how that character felt)

- What would you like to do next?

- How do you plan to capture that story?

- What tools do you need?

- I look forward to hearing more!

And here are some other considerations to keep in mind:

- How might working with this story with a new material support the language and the idea to grow?

- Is the child interested in publishing the story? Is publishing an expectation you have for the work you are doing with the whole group?

- What kind of support with writing conventions does the child need? How will you best support those needs? What tools can you offer?

- Is this child doing something that other children might benefit from as a model? If so, how might you encourage that child to share what they've done with the group, perhaps during story sharing? (See Chapter 6.)

We encourage you to explore the video collection for Chapter 5 in the online resources, which features teachers working alongside children during story creation.

Pictures of Practice
Supporting a Child's Intention

During the first week of school in a kindergarten and first-grade class-room, one material that was available for story creation was watercolor palettes. Their teacher was curious to see how they would use this material and what stories it would inspire. She was focused on getting to know them and wanted to gather more information about what they were interested in and curious about. She was surprised when instead of painting on the watercolor paper, the children became more engaged in what happened when they dabbed their paintbrushes on the blotter. The way the colors spread through the paper towel fibers sparked something in their imaginations, and they spent their time making what they called tie-dye on the blotters. At first, the teacher was concerned. She reflected, "It wasn't my intention for them to use the materials in that way and I found myself at first wanting to shut it down. After observing what the children were doing, and wanting to support their intention, even if I didn't fully understand or agree with it, I decided to give them a nudge to write about it." Her decision to listen to the children and respond with what she considered an appropriate next step led the children to write books titled, "How to Make Tie-Dye." As they worked on the steps for making tie-dye, they realized that although the books had the same title, each author was making different decisions about the steps to include in their book. They celebrated the decisions they were making as authors and had opportunities to teach classmates how to make tie-dye by sharing the books they wrote.

Drafting "How to Make Tie-Dye"

Reflection

Dyson writes: "Children's interest in one kind of symbol making, writing, is best viewed within the context of children's artistic and social lives, as that writing is couched within their drawing, talking, and playing. . . . Adults can help connect print with the liveliness of children's use of other symbolic forms" (1990, 56). How would you describe the ways the teacher in the previous "Pictures of Practice" story supported the children to connect print to their use of other forms? What was gained?

Where do the three dispositions of citizen world-makers you are focused on show up here?

The Power of Play

Of course, the arts and story are inseparable from play. Children play, so they think, so they talk, so they connect, and on it goes. Play and story help us explore the uncertainties of the perceptual ecologies in which we live. The arts help us find and make meaning for ourselves and for others. The arts and story and

play are all critical tools that we use to ignite and fuel the fire of imagination that is our birthright as human beings. They are all ways in which we turn the chaos of what is possible to perceive in our environment into something we understand, can share, and can act on. Play and art and story are tools that allow us to experiment with life and to take charge of it. Given the primacy of this evolutionary survival strategy, we needn't worry that children are playing too much in school. We need to worry that they aren't playing enough. We need to create opportunities for ourselves to witness the power of play in our classrooms so that we can advocate for its place in school as a critical tool for learning. We need to document it. So instead of spending a lot of words here making the case for play, I'll cut right to the chase: to deny the right to play is to deny a most basic human right. William Ayers writes powerfully about the implications of this loss in our schools:

> **Too many schools, day in and day out, are organized to smash curiosity, impede imagination, shatter self-respect, and deflate the dreams of youth. They reward obedience and compliance while punishing creativity and courage, initiative and ingenuity. This is the brutal masquerade called school offered to the descendants of formerly enslaved human beings, First Nation peoples, and immigrants from colonized communities. For these mostly Black and Brown and poor kids, the classroom marches under the gauzy banner of enlightenment and democracy, empowerment and progress, while operating relentlessly to reproduce and police the hierarchies of winners and losers along predictable lines of race and class. These American schools have inequity and congealed violence baked into their DNA. (2019, 4)**

The achievement gap is an opportunity gap created by a system that operates from within a deficit paradigm in which some people are deemed deficient and therefore unworthy of school environments that create conditions to nurture the unique genius of the creative, inquisitive, storytelling brain that every human being carries inside them (Chakrabarti, Carter, and Kendi 2019). The paradigm that sustains these attitudes is "baked" into the story of the United States, past and present. This system is convenient for those who control it. It holds the line between those who produce ideas and those that only reproduce ideas (Moss 2014). Teachers play an important role in reimagining that story and removing that boundary.

Play is so important for healthy brain development and well-being that it is listed in the United Nations Convention on the Rights of the Child, which has been ratified in every country in the world, with the notable exception of the United States (Rothschild 2017). Early childhood development scholars and pediatricians overwhelmingly agree that children learn best when they are engaged and enjoying themselves (Ginsburg 2007). *All* children. Zaretta Hammond (2015) writes about the learning brain's need to be in an environment where it can enter a state of "relaxed alertness," a key element of culturally responsive practice and the state of mind achieved in play. In their book *Bridging Literacy and Equity: The Essential Guide to Social Equity Teaching*, Lazar, Edwards, and McMillon write:

> **Learning is more likely to happen when there are socially compelling reasons to do so, when the learning environment is comfortable. . . . On the other hand, when the learning environment is stressful and adversarial, Krashen suggests that learners raise an affective filter that works to block learning. This can happen when students are called out and told that their language is "incorrect" or "needs to be fixed." . . . Educators need to validate the language that students bring from home and establish meaningful, supportive, and motivating conditions. (2012, 57)**

In story workshop, what matters is the story and the conditions that invited that story and all the emotion it holds to overflow the mind. Children will write. Children want to write when we make sure it is socially compelling to do so. The use of symbols to construct meaning and relationship in the world is primal. So how can we create schools that are accountable for supporting children in realizing *their* intentions rather than testing them relentlessly on the extent to which they have helped us achieve our own? Teachers who are drawing out and listening to and working with the stories of the children who are right in front of them will show us how.

Loris Malaguzzi, the founder of the pedagogical approach used in the municipally funded preprimary schools in Reggio Emilia, Italy, envisioned "a new type of school made of spaces where the hands of children could be active for messing about. With no possibility of boredom, the hands and minds would engage each other with great, liberating merriment in a way ordained by biology and evolution" (in Edwards, Gandini, and Forman 2012, 49). The rich, diverse, aesthetically rewarding school environments in Reggio Emilia have inspired educators around the world to aspire to an improved aesthetic experience for children. And that's a fine thing. But it is vital to understand that these experiences are a response to what we have learned about what has been "ordained by biology and evolution." That is the important thing. To deny these environments and experiences within them is to deny what we know about what it takes for human beings to thrive.

Reflection: *A Dialogue with Materials*

Search online for Mary Oliver's poem "Wild Geese" and read it, or find a link to her reading it aloud (https://soundcloud.com/onbeing/wild-geese-by-mary-oliver).
Choose a material to work with as you reflect on these questions:

- What if every child who arrived at school found it to be a place where they were welcomed into the family of things?

- How do you feel when you are told that you do not have to be good?

- In what ways does the world offer itself to our imagination?

- What can we do to ensure that children believe that to be true?

Take out your journal and record words that capture your thoughts. Consider your chosen three words.

Make a commitment to one action inspired by these thoughts.

Pictures of Practice
Celebrating and Sustaining Uncertainty

Play, as a way to make sense of information through experimentation with possibility in story workshop, is for everyone. We all—teachers and children—need to practice our practice with the understanding that true mastery doesn't come as we arrive at a predetermined destination but instead from the ability to carry on knowing that there isn't one (Lewis 2014). Play makes that ongoing journey possible, tolerable, and joyful. Efforts to corner certainty, on the other hand, strand us on a mountaintop, limiting our options for further exploration. The following story provides a view from both perspectives.

Violet joined her new school as a first grader, in a classroom of returning first and second graders who had experience with story workshop. When the teachers invited her to tell a story using materials for the first time, she looked at them like they were crazy. Being invited to play with materials was unfamiliar and seemed to create a risk she didn't imagine to be worth taking.

According to her family, Violet had been introduced to writing workshop in kindergarten, and making books was a familiar activity that she enjoyed. Making books is an expectation during story workshop, too, and in Figures 5.1a–d, you can see the pages of a book she made during the first weeks of school.

The teachers were delighted that Violet chose to write a book about herself. It helped them get to know her and made traces of her thinking visible within the classroom. It helped them assess her strengths as a writer. But they continued to be curious about her reluctance to engage with other materials.

> "If we split practice from the real thing, neither one of them will be very real."
>
> —Stephen Nachmanovitch, *Free Play: Improvisation in Life and the Arts* (2015, 67)

They wondered if Violet's comfort with bookmaking could be the reason she was resistant to stepping beyond that comfort zone. Yes, she could produce a book. She could do it willingly and happily and with the kind of confidence that came from believing she knew how to do it right. She was certain, and it was likely that her efforts had been celebrated in the past, so she was comfortable. After all, Beau Lotto writes, "uncertainty is *the* problem our brains evolved to solve" (2017, 8), because the alternative—fumbling around in an environment we can't make sense of—is a dangerous thing to do. That discomfort of not knowing was evident to the teachers as they observed Violet's behavior. Jennifer Eberhardt's (2020) research on bias confirms this need to resolve uncertainty and makes the case that it comes at a cost. Lotto (2017) agrees: that cost is our freedom. Imposing rigid rules insulates us from the complexity of the ecology in which we live. What we trade for that comfort is a limitation on and even elimination of our capacity for courage, creativity, connection, or collaboration. To put aside the complexity of our experiences for a school day is to limit the practice we need to learn to accept it, to be curious about it, and to develop the tools we need to manage ourselves in the midst of it.

The teachers continued to focus on encouraging Violet to explore a variety of media as she played with and alongside her peers.

A few weeks later, the teachers asked the children to pick a story to take through a publication process. It could be one they'd already started or one they hadn't yet found. Violet struggled to find her story—and this was the

struggle the teachers hoped she'd have. Sacks writes, "To be ourselves we must *have* ourselves—possess, if need be re-possess, our life-stories. We must 'recollect' ourselves, recollect the inner drama, the narrative, of ourselves. A man needs such a narrative, a continuous inner narrative, to maintain his identity, his self" (in Popova 2018). The teachers hoped this moment of disequilibrium and indecision would create an opportunity to discover the potential of the materials to shake loose something she cared about from within her imagination—a way to recollect herself. They invited her to join her friend Chloe in the blocks.

And because it is what happens when children play, it wasn't long before Violet and Chloe found a story. Violet liked the story but not enough to make a book out of it yet. So the teachers were surprised when the next morning, Violet burst into the classroom with a huge smile on her face. Before they could even say, "Hello," Violet exclaimed, "I found my story!" She got right to work, diving in with an enthusiasm and energy they hadn't yet seen from her.

Images on the next page offer a peek into what it looked like.

Not incidentally, it seemed that in becoming responsible for finding her own story rather than for the task of writing, she'd developed a whole lot of writing skill.

Learning from peers

Looking for a story with blocks

Later, when her teachers asked Violet about her story, she advised them, "If you follow your dreams, you'll find a land where there are real fairies." A learning community that values discomfort with certainty creates conditions that ensure all children have an opportunity to understand this for themselves, in their own way. It's a community that encourages the people that show up there to do the things they do in whatever way they do them by giving them tools and time to do them. It's through the journey to that land that we hope to walk alongside them, asking questions, listening, connecting, and believing they can.

Standardized expectations are stories that rely on us to tell them, coercing children to believe their unique experiences and interpretations of the world exist on a spectrum of good and right. Our efforts to rewrite those stories for ourselves invite children to know that stories that exclude or marginalize them *must* be rewritten, and they have the tools they need to get where they want to go.

Action Steps: Enrich Your Story Workshop Practice

🖋 If you believe children should have more opportunity to play in school, create time for yourself to document what happens when they do. Use research from the Alliance for Childhood, the American Academy of Pediatrics, the Lego Foundation, or Project Zero to substantiate your findings, and share them. Make your own learning visible. Host an evening for parents to discuss. Create an advocacy group of parents and teachers to demand more time to play in school.

🖋 If you are uncertain about the balance between academic work and play during story workshop, experiment with what happens when you create various boundaries. What happens if everyone writes one day? What happens if no one writes one day and everyone works with materials? What happens if you allow children to choose their own boundaries for a week? What happens if you zoom in on one child or one group of children and consider these boundaries? Try things. Document what happens. Reflect. And try again.

🖋 If you're concerned about the issue of bias, read Dr. Jennifer Eberhardt's book *Biased: Uncovering the Hidden Prejudice That Shapes What We See, Think, and Do* (2020). Host a book group to discuss.

EDUCATOR INTERVIEW: SHARING OUR LIVED REALITY

Excerpted from an interview with Rosemarie Biocarles-Rydeen, kindergarten teacher, High Tech Elementary School, Chula Vista, California

AT OUR SCHOOL WE HAVE CHILDREN THAT ARE REPRESENTED FROM all parts of South Bay, San Diego. We have a large percentage of English learners because of our proximity to the Mexico border. I was curious about how I could be true to play as a catalyst for language and literacy learning, and that's how the story workshop approach ended up in my classroom.

Because we already use a project-based approach and that felt familiar, the first time I tried story workshop, I decided to turn it into a project with a focus on storytelling. Our project would explore the understanding that we *all* have stories to share and what connects us as human beings is stories.

I sent an email out to the whole staff and to families to invite people in to share stories. When people came, there was always so much interest in sharing and hearing other people's stories. Once they were so immersed in story, I started introducing different materials.

What I really love about the approach is that it pulls everything together. If we create the conditions to seek and share and connect over stories, then, I find, the engagement for the phonics is there. All those other pieces of literacy lessons are all pulled together because, ultimately, they're going to support us when we're trying to share our story!

I can think of two instances when children had what might be considered writing block. I invited one of them, Caleb, to spend some time with clay. After some time and some messing around, I checked in with him. He had made a little ladder out of clay, but he said, "I'm still not sure."

So I encouraged him to keep working with it. "I know that a story will wake up!"

Rosemarie at work

I checked again a bit later and there was a figure on the ladder. I asked, "What's going on here?"

And he said, "Well, this kind of reminds me of the time that I went to the park. I went across the monkey bars all by myself!" It's so amazing to see a child with what seemed like a little bit of learned helplessness come up with his own story just by spending some time with clay.

Another child, Dante, struggled to find a story at one point. He also wanted to work with clay. He suddenly said, "This is an island."

I said, "OK, now you've got a setting for your story. What's going to happen there?"

He said, "I don't know." At that moment, another child, Ruby, wandered by. They started talking and before I knew it Dante was spinning a tale about a person on the island who got eaten by a dinosaur! This story became a book titled "The Island," which was one of the best-reviewed books by the other children all year. Just time with clay and talking to Ruby and then—*snap*—he got it. He got an idea. The clay reminded him of something. Materials and some time to play and talk to friends really are the best tools for bringing forward the very work we so strongly believe children need to do—and have a right to do. Why have we spent so much time fighting their natural instincts? I wonder how much of the deficits we see in children are because they just can't fight that fight. We lose so many children like Dante and Ruby and Caleb that way.

Honoring the relational and creative capacity of children by giving them materials, because we know they can go there when they are given the right tools, is the most important takeaway from my experience with story workshop so far. I feel that by taking the word *writer* out of the workshop, we turn it into a bigger idea: that we all connect as human beings through stories.

And the children see it. They're like, "Oh my gosh, stories are everywhere!"

And I'm like, "I know. That movie you're watching? It's a story. That show you're watching? It's a story."

And they're like, "Oh my gosh, my painting is a story!"

Story workshop gives us a way to share our lived reality.

●●●●●●●●●●●●●●●●

"You don't have to just revise stories!
You can revise what you think, too. Like,
your ideas and what you think is true!
You have to be flexible in your brain."

—Evelyn (age 6)

●●●●●●●●●●●●●●●●

CHAPTER SIX
Story Sharing

Each session of story workshop ends with a whole-group reflection on the work that happened during story creation, called story sharing. Story sharing *also* refers to any time during story workshop that is dedicated to reflection, revision, or dialogue about a child's work or a project in which a small group or the whole group is engaged. Following is a little glimpse of story sharing.

The children gathered for snack and sharing. It was Simon's turn to share his new story. Sarah asked him what he wanted to hear from his audience, and Simon asked for "connections." Here's part of the dialogue:

> **Simon:** I want people to have connections because it feels good to me.
>
> **Sarah:** Yeah, if people can connect to something about you or something you've done, that feels really good. Is that true for anybody else?
>
> **Vivian:** It feels good because people know something about me.
>
> **Sarah:** Does anyone have a connection to Simon's story?

See Video 6.1 to take a peek into how this story workshop session came full circle.

Video 6.1 Sharing: Children Ages 5–7

See page ix on how to access this video.

151

What Is Story Sharing? Learning to Listen

Story workshop ends each day with story sharing—a journey to explore the territory of understanding, imagination, curiosity, and empathy. It's a time for zooming in, paying attention, listening, and making connections. In the words of five-year-old Tristan, "the power of a story is to bring you something new if it's in something in you or something in the world." Story sharing is a place where that power is in force.

Story sharing can take many forms, which we'll explore in this chapter, but it is always focused on reflection, dialogue, and listening.

If you already make time in your classroom for children to share their work with one another—as I think you probably do—this chapter will give you more good reasons to keep it up. If you don't yet take time for children to share, this chapter will provide support to get started. You don't need anything fancy—no collections of materials, no intricate classroom designs. Listening to the stories children tell (whether they've created them during story workshop or during some other structure you use) can inform your decisions about other parts of the workshop structure that you'd like to explore or enhance—and those decisions will be even more effective because they are grounded in the children's stories themselves.

Three- and four-year-olds and their teacher look at stories based on loose-parts collage during story sharing. Those with their hands up, including the teacher, are signaling that they have a connection with the author.

Pictures of Practice
Zooming in to Understand

Sarah, a kindergarten and first-grade teacher at Opal School, shares and reflects on an experience she had with children in her classroom:

> As I observed children beginning to wonder about perspective and overheard them play with ideas about how things in nature might see the world, I wondered how slowing down and zooming in on the details of collected natural materials might help us. The children practiced blind contour drawing and used clay to replicate texture and shape of a chosen material—a shell, a pine cone, a fern. We spent over a week using materials to practice slowing down and really looking, using the same object for several days at a time. This was as hard as you imagine it was! Because there is such value in slowing down, returning to something over time, and trying to capture what we see, I knew these five- to seven-year-old children could do this and that our work would benefit from it. But to be sure we had a shared value, I asked the children why they thought it was important for humans to slow down and notice. Here is a snippet of their conversation:

> > **Alex:** If you don't zoom in, then you don't really know what something looks like.
> >
> > **Astrid:** You might miss something important!
> >
> > **Evelyn:** Yeah, and people like to know what things are!
> >
> > **Teo:** And people like to learn.
> >
> > **William:** They are curious.
> >
> > **Alex:** If you never look closely, you might be scared of something when you don't need to be! Just because you don't understand.
> >
> > **Sam:** Yeah, and humans just want to understand life on Earth! We want to understand why. Zooming in helps us understand why.

Astrid: Well . . . when you zoom in, you might understand parts that you didn't before. And life is kind of like what you feel. If you understand what something feels, you kind of understand part of its life.

In my experience, reflection leads to greater understanding. In this instance, reflection allowed the children to begin playing with the relationship between slowing down, paying attention, curiosity, and empathy. They spontaneously drew connections between looking closely at the objects and looking closely at each other. Through dialogue and reflection, the children shared their way into a big question that I was curious about as well: What is the connection between understanding, imagination, curiosity, and empathy?

Reflection

How does this story relate to the three words you chose to focus on as dispositions of citizen world-makers?

Writing Workshop Connection: *Share Time or Author's Chair*

The structure of writing workshop generally ends with time to share, usually five to fifteen minutes. Sometimes it looks like one child sitting in an author's chair, sharing a finished piece of writing. Sometimes it looks like one child sharing a piece of writing in order to get feedback from peers in the form of compliments, questions, or suggestions. Sometimes the teacher asks a few students to share with the whole class what they tried in their own writing from the minilesson that day and helps other children envision what that might look like in their own writing. Sometimes small pairs or groups of students share from their ongoing work. During this time, children and teachers work to develop an understanding of what it means to write within a community of authors who support one another.

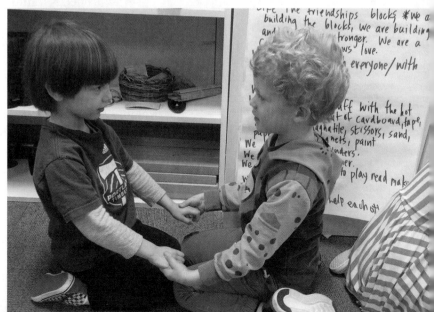

Making Time and Space for Sharing: The Teacher's Role

Story sharing at the end of story workshop is a short period of time, usually scheduled for about fifteen minutes, give or take a few. A lot of big things can happen in that short amount of time, so it's helpful to be thoughtful and organized about the ways in which individual experiences connect to and expand the whole. Using the work of the children themselves, story sharing becomes an opportunity to build community, to practice listening and making connections, to inspire children to take on new challenges, to synthesize ideas, and to expand imagination.

Knowing that a sharing time, responsive to what the children are working on, is planned into the schedule each day of story workshop means that we are often planning for story sharing during story creation. We might ask ourselves:

- What child, or children, will offer the most inspiration, challenge, provocation, or helpful model for the others?

- What group of authors' work will provide the most productive collection of models or contrasts on any given day?

- Who needs a boost of confidence?

- Who wants to share? Who is reluctant to share?

- Who made particularly interesting use of that day's provocation?

- Who had an important insight to share?

- Who needs a nudge?

- Who needs a chance to celebrate?

Typically, it's helpful to make a quick plan with the child or children you ask to share. Take care that children have equitable opportunity to share over time, and keep records to track who shares from day to day so that everyone gets roughly equal time over the course of a week or two. You can add these notes to the memory keeping tool you choose to use. (See Figure 4.3 for the Weekly Memory Keeping tool, also available in Online Resource 4.1.)

When children volunteer to share, as they often do, find ways to accommodate that desire. You might try one of these strategies:

- Ask what they think they need from sharing and find ways to connect that need to the priorities of the whole that day.

- Ask the child to consider sharing with a small group or a "brain buddy."

- Ask the child to wait for another day.

- Consider whether it might work for the child to share during provocation at the next session of story workshop.

- Say, "Yes!"

We actively seek connections to relevant skills, strategies, content, questions, and interests throughout the sharing structure. As you listen, consider these questions:

- How might we use one child's story or process to reflect on a strategy that all children will benefit from?

- How might I use a listener's question or connection to a story to highlight skills or strategies we hope to learn?

- How can my participation encourage and sustain divergent thinking within the group so that both identity and community are strengthened?

- Where are there opportunities to reflect on the role of play, collaboration, or the use of the arts?

- Where are my opportunities to nurture listening and response?

A three-year-old shares a story with his teacher.

🍃 How can I stay open to surprise?

🍃 How will this sharing influence preparation and provocation for tomorrow?

Of course, we need to consider what logistical support a particular group of children might benefit from at any given time. You might ask yourself:

🍃 Who are these children and what will best support them to take charge of their sharing and listening?

🍃 What kind of seating works best?

🍃 Does it help to have fidget toys available?

🍃 Is sharing time a good time for children to eat a snack?

🍃 What experiences will help the children learn to choose smart spots (seats on the floor in which they will find the least distraction) or understand what it means to be a brain buddy?

Connecting, Reflecting, and Giving Feedback: The Children's Role

The central intent of story sharing is for children to engage with each other's stories. To make this time as significant and useful as possible, children need support in learning how to meaningfully connect with each other and to give feedback, and they need to practice these exchanges. What happens between the children is as important—and arguably more so (Mikkelson 1990)—as the stories themselves. In addition to offering perspective on the stories, sharing is how children make sense of their interconnectedness as a group (Dyson and Genishi 1994). During story sharing, we encourage children to

- ask questions of one another,
- pay attention and ask for clarifications,
- listen carefully enough to care,
- say what they've noticed and how they feel, and
- offer suggestions, more ideas, and connections.

We can facilitate children's capacity to engage in story sharing by focusing on connection. It takes time to learn to listen deeply. With this understanding in mind, teachers frequently ask questions such as these:

- Who was reminded of their own story?
- What pictures did you make in your mind?
- What are you wondering?
- How did the story make you feel?
- Do you have any connections?
- What inspired you?

Most importantly, we model engaged listening ourselves. We share the emotions and connections we have with the story. Instead of taking control of the behavior of the group, teachers support children to participate in the development of community norms. This works best when there is ample time to reflect and construct a genuine sense of what works when it comes to sharing for your particular students in your particular classroom. In order to support a culture of listening, reflect together on the sharing experience itself. You might ask:

- What does listening sound like, look like, and feel like?

- How do you feel when someone listens to you?

- How did you feel when your friends listened to your story?

- Does it feel like everyone is listening now?

- Did it feel like everyone listened? What felt good? What could have felt better?

- What might we do differently next time?

Often, teachers organize story sharing as an opportunity to reflect on story workshop as a whole. In place of sharing stories, from time to time, you might ask the children questions such as these:

- How did it feel today during story creation time? Are there things we should keep doing or stop doing?

- Where do your ideas come from?

- What do you do when you get stuck?

- Why do you think it feels so good when your story is heard?

- How do materials help you tell stories?

- What does a connection feel like?

- Why do people tell stories?

- Does listening look different for different people?

- How do we support differences in listening and being listened to, and how can we work together to make story workshop a place where all stories are welcome?

None of these questions has a definitive answer. They are intended to generate possibility and to gently nurture a discomfort with certainty. These questions require adults who are ready to ask them because they are curious about what will happen when they do. Year over year, we will ask the same or similar questions, knowing that the responses will be new. They are new because the children are different and the times are different and, critically, because the teacher's world has expanded with another year of living under the influence of listening—and so, year over year, the teacher hears more and hears differently. As your sense of possibility expands, so does your perception, so does your imagination, so does your sense of wonder. Vivian Gussin Paley writes of her own experience of coming to recognize that before she began listening carefully to the stories the children told, she had a habit of confusing "the extraordinary with the mundane" (2004, 72). As we learn to turn down the volume of our adult agendas, we find ourselves better prepared to be immersed in the astonishing capacity of young children's drive to make meaning as individuals in order to create a world to which they belong.

More Ways to Share Stories

Sharing can take many forms and may include a variety of modes of expression. Children can act out each other's stories with costumes or props or pure imagination. They can read or dance or share a set of paintings.

Opportunities to share and celebrate with families strengthen the connections within a community.

Sharing can take place just between a teacher and a child. It can take place between two children who are invited to sit close and facing one another. It can take place as part of a publishing celebration or when a piece is in its very early stages—when an author is finished or stuck or has barely begun. Story sharing might work best one day with small groups of students and another day with the whole group. Some days it can happen at the beginning of the workshop in order to provide the day's provocation.

We tell stories in order to connect with other people. Sharing our stories is the heart of story workshop, so it doesn't need to be restricted to the end! (Take a look at Online Resource Videos 6.2 through 6.4. They are associated with this chapter and Chapter 3. I think you'll see how these sharing moments might have been used as provocations to open the day's workshop.)

Video 6.2 Sharing: Children Ages 3–5

Video 6.3 Sharing: Children Ages 6–8

Video 6.4 Gray's Lemon Poem: Children Ages 6–8

See page ix on how to access these videos.

Pictures of Practice
Finding Belonging in a New Community Through Sharing

During his first month of kindergarten, five-year-old Asher decided to use small blocks to find a new story. (See the following two images.). As he played, he found an idea for a story about a rocket ship. He happily used a blank book to capture the story he made up as he played. After he spent story creation this way for two days, his teacher, Sarah, thought that he would benefit from sharing with the whole group and asked him if he would be willing. She knew that sharing would clarify and help strengthen his engagement with his story, and through story, sharing would strengthen his relationship to his new community.

Asher agreed and shared his first two pages with the whole group. When other children asked what might happen next, he was unsure and seemed to be feeling ready to move on. Sarah suggested that he might ask for ideas from his classmates about what could happen next. When Milo said, "Maybe

someone could die and someone is really sad about it," and, laughing, added, "Then . . . they could come back alive again!" Asher smiled, nodded his head, and started laughing, too.

He added on to Milo's idea: "Or ghosts could fly out of it!"

Milo nodded in agreement and then suggested a way Asher could find out more about the story: "Tomorrow, you could put fabric over you. That would turn you into a ghost."

Asher couldn't wait to go back to his story to add the part that he and Milo had thought up. Ultimately, Asher decided his story was a silly one where aliens arrived and turned a person into a "dogface human." He was full of giggles as he went around the room to share his silly ending—and he delighted everyone.

In the weeks following this experience, Sarah noticed that Asher engaged with one idea for longer periods of time, that he was eager to share with his peers, and that he began asking his family to come into the classroom regularly so that he could share his stories with them. Asher clearly signaled that, through sharing his story with others, he felt valued, appreciated, and understood in ways that served to increase his desire to participate in his own work as well as in the life of the community.

Sharing Stories Weaves a Web
of Community and Belonging

The experience of Asher is simple, really. As it is for Paul, or Stella, or Scouten, or Sam. As it is for the children of the teachers interviewed as part of this book project. As it is for so many other teachers who have found a way for children to explore materials, to play, to author stories, and to share. Our experience in the world compels us to reach out to others to find connection and belonging. We play out our individual tales on the stage of the world and in the process learn more about both.

Anne Haas Dyson and Celia Genishi write,

> **The storytelling self is a social self, who declares and shapes important relationships through the mediating power of words. Thus, in sharing stories, we have the potential for forging new relationships, including local, classroom "cultures" in which individuals are interconnected and new "we's" formed. . . . At the same time, those very images and rhythms reverberate in the memories of audience members, who reconstruct the story with the stuff of their own thoughts and feelings. In such ways, individual lives are woven together through the stuff of stories. (1994, 5)**

Asher's story helps us see this powerful, simple, beautifully complex process in action. When we embrace that complexity, and develop strategies to tolerate the inherent uncertainty that our stories land within others in ways we can never fully understand, we build an expectation for diversity and we recognize that we are healthy and thriving because of it. Reflecting together through sharing stories is an important part of building connections across difference in ways that celebrate rather than work to eradicate it. "Homogeneity is fine in a bottle of milk, but in the classroom it diminishes the curiosity that ignites discovery" (Paley 1979, 53).

As I've discussed in earlier chapters, children grow within a complex ecology. Their perceptual experience both constrains and releases their imagination; what they perceive within that ecology becomes what they think, what they do, and what they share (Lotto 2017). An idea, a theory, or a story can only grow from experience, and the strength of the idea, the theory, or the story is reliant on the way in which that experience is experienced. The methods we use to learn about the world cannot be disentangled from the world itself.

Vivian Gussin Paley reflected on her teaching before she began truly listening to children—and all that is lost when we don't: "I rarely paused to listen to the narratives blooming everywhere in the garden of children in which I spent my days. I saw myself as the bestower of place and belonging, of custom and curriculum, too often ignoring the delicate web being constructed by the children in their constant exchange of ideas the moment I stopped talking and they resumed playing" (2004, 73).

It is a delicate web, this ecology that constructs us as we construct it. It is delicate because of the primal need, in the development of human beings, for a sense of belonging. We literally cannot survive without it, and this is as true in a big-picture evolutionary sense as it is with the birth of each new person. Evolution equipped children to be competent in the most important

ways—specifically, in their ability to connect with the world. When they are born, they don't know the world, of course, but they have everything they need to come to know it and, in the process, themselves. The version of the world that adults offer has powerful influence over what children come to know about themselves.

Children have the tools they need. But they will sacrifice them all for belonging. They'll give up curiosity if being wrong risks alienation. They'll give up creativity if being right ensures a place in the group. They'll give up imagination if their ideas don't have influence. So the task before us is to create a classroom culture in which no one risks alienation, in which everyone's ideas have influence, and to which everyone believes that they belong. Story sharing creates this opportunity each day.

In her book *On Looking*, Alexandra Horowitz writes, "I reckon that every child has been admonished to 'pay attention.' But no one tells you how" (2013, 9). This common childhood dilemma puts at risk the agency needed to see the world with a fresh perspective. It endangers the confidence that what *we* are paying attention to might have meaning to others as well. We learn to distrust our own eyes and ears. Horowitz writes, "To the newborn infant, there is no 'crib,' no 'mama' and 'daddy,' no floor no wall no window no sky. Much of this can be seen, but none can yet be made sense of" (2013, 22). As we have seen, the sense making is primal. And it relies in an irreducible way on the order and organization imposed by those around us. "The child begins by having to match what can be seen with what cannot be seen—the experience of other people who have created his language and culture" (Cobb 1993, 47–48). Children are continually working to make that match, so our efforts to direct their attention should be made with care and with a sober understanding that regardless of whether we realize we are pointing, children will follow. We nurture what we model.

To be clear, I am not advocating the replacement of one culture with another, or to turn any established hierarchy on its head, but to connect, genuinely, with the lives of diverse children who need and want and have a right to remain themselves as much as they need and want and have a right to be part of the group (Greene, in Dyson and Genishi 1994). We want to establish a culture in which we can negotiate meaning together. That is the work. So let's be clear here: story sharing, as part of story workshop, is intended to create a disruption to the status quo. It is intended to give children practice with the following:

- maintaining a healthy relationship with authority that strengthens democracy

- navigating difference and multiple perspectives

- making connections and nurturing a sense of belonging

- tolerating uncertainty and sustaining ambiguity

- working through conflict, self-regulation, and various emotions

- using civic and social imagination

Learning to Listen

Somewhat ironically, story sharing is wholly reliant on story listening. The opportunity to practice the things listed in the previous section is created *because of* that reciprocity. In an essay titled "On Listening to What the Children Say," Vivian Gussin Paley (1986) reflects on the development of her ability to listen to what children are trying to say in order to establish a culture where everyone is making meaning—adults and children together. She describes an encounter with a high school teacher named Bill who had asked if he could spend some time in Paley's classroom. Here is some of what she observed of his interactions with the children:

> He asked a question or made a casual observation, then repeated each child's comment and hung onto it until a link was made to someone else's idea. Together they were constructing a paper chain of magical imaginings mixed with some solid facts, and Bill was providing the glue.

But something else was going on that was essential to Bill's success. He was truly curious. He had few expectations of what five-year-olds might say or think, and he listened to their responses with the anticipation one brings to the theater when a mystery is being revealed. Bill was interested not in what he knew to be an answer, but only in how the children intuitively approached a problem. . . .

I began to copy Bill's style whenever the children and I had formal discussions. I practiced his open-ended questions, the kind that seek no specific answers but rather build a chain of ideas without the need for closure. It was not easy. I felt myself always waiting for the right answer—my answer. The children knew I was waiting and watched my face for clues. Clearly, it was not enough simply to copy someone else's teaching manner; real change comes about only through the painful recognition of one's own vulnerability. (123)

If we are to truly enter that space where the reciprocity lives between sharing and listening, we will make ourselves vulnerable, and that's always a hard place to be. Paley found the use of audio recording to be of particular support as she learned to cope with that painful recognition in the context of her work with children.

Try This: *Learning to Listen*

Create an opportunity for the children in your care to talk with you. This could be a whole-group or small-group experience. It could involve sharing a story written by a child or reading a story by a distant author. It could be a moment of play alongside children in the block or dramatic play area. Any moment of extended conversation will do.

Record the conversation. We find that using a phone makes this easy. The use of a voice memo is fine, but we also like a variety of apps (AudioNote, Evernote, and Notability, to name a few) that not only record but also support transcription.

Transcribe the conversation word for word.

Then ask yourself some questions:

- Read back over the transcription. What do you notice? What stands out to you? What questions do you have?

- Look for places in the transcript that you read differently than what you thought you had heard being spoken at the time. What surprised you?

- Look at the places where you intervened. See if you can articulate why you did that. What was going on in your mind? How do you think your interventions shifted the conversation?

- Look at the places where you listened without speaking. What were you thinking in those moments? What connections were you making? What questions did you have?

- Where might you have asked an open-ended question? Where might you have made an observation? Where might you have repeated a child's comment in order to help them make connections?

- Were there moments when you found yourself waiting for a "right" answer? What do you predict you missed by doing this?

- What patterns do you notice come up within the dialogue? What questions do you hear the children asking (even if they're not in the form of a question)?

- What are you left feeling genuinely curious about?

- What quote or snippet of dialogue might you bring back to the children in order to get more information, continue to build understanding, seek connections, or encourage reflection?

Story Sharing Creates Mirrors and Opens Windows

The ecology of a child's perceptual experience extends, of course, beyond the classroom to all the environments in which that child has perceptual encounters of any kind. The stories children have to share will represent connections between their lives in and out of school. Children are making meaning of all of it and do not leave experiences behind as they enter and exit the school—and nor do teachers. For some children and adults, however, those transitions are more dissonant than for others. Dr. Debbie Reese, who founded the blog *American Indians in Children's*

Literature, writes: "When you're the parent of a Native or child of color, your child's identity is not affirmed in the ways that the identity of white children is" (2019). The infographic in Figure 6.1 backs up her statement.

Sarah Park Dahlen (2019), who contributed to the development of this infographic, explains the choice of the cracked mirrors: "We made a deliberate decision to crack a section of the children's mirrors to indicate what Debbie Reese calls 'funhouse mirrors' and Ebony Elizabeth Thomas calls 'distorted funhouse mirrors of the self.' Children's literature continues to misrepresent underrepresented communities, and we wanted this infographic to show not just the low quantity of existing literature, but also the inaccuracy and uneven quality of some of those books." The mirror metaphor was inspired by Rudine Sims Bishop, who wrote,

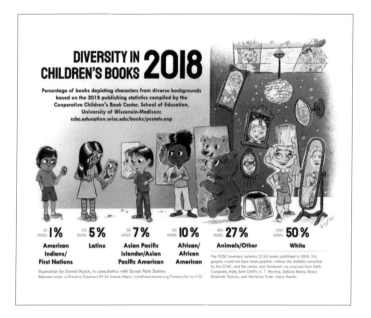

Figure 6.1 Diversity in Children's Books 2018 (Huyck and Dahlen 2019)

> Children from dominant social groups have always found their mirrors in books, but they, too, have suffered from the lack of availability of books about others. They need the books as windows onto reality, not just on imaginary worlds. They need books that will help them understand the multicultural nature of the world they live in, and their place as a member of just one group, as well as their connections to all other humans. In this country, where racism is still one of the major unresolved social problems, books may be one of the few places where children who are socially isolated and insulated from the larger world may meet people unlike themselves. If they see only reflections of themselves, they will grow up with an exaggerated sense of their own importance and value in the world—a dangerous ethnocentrism. (2015)

Although the problem of unequal representation is significant and requires significant advocacy, I think that while we wait for those statistics to change, we can take responsibility for creating the conditions in which children craft and share their own stories (and in so doing, hurry along the change in the world).

"Hearing other people's ideas helped me to feel visible again."

—Evelyn (age 6)

Jacqueline Woodson (2019) talks about the importance of this process in her TED talk "What Reading Slowly Taught Me About Writing." In her own words, she describes the experience of making that match between what is seen and not seen. She says, "You begin to question because it's adults and it's their gaze. That's the mirror for you." There is so much unseen in that gaze, whether it comes from parents or teachers or television or books or the president or peers. The unseen is what you begin to see in yourself. Woodson says her response was to write her own stories. "They didn't exist when I was growing up. I grew up in Bushwick and I was like: *Where are the books about a black girl growing up in Bushwick in the home of a single mom and whose best friend is Puerto Rican and so who grew up speaking Spanish and English?* I wanted to tell those stories. . . . I was indignant, like, *How dare the world not have my narrative in it?*" When asked, "Who gave you that sense, like, *Hello, you all need to hear my story, too!?*" she said it was because of this: "My family saying, 'You matter.' I came out of Jim Crow South—from South Carolina to New York City—and so I think somewhere along all those lines, people were saying, 'You matter.' And then to hear all your life you matter and you're amazing and you're brilliant and you're beautiful and then to not see that in the world, it's like, wait a second—I mean, I know my people weren't lying. So America must be lying."

Making time for story sharing tells children, "You matter," because they know their classroom is a place where their own stories have influence. They strengthen the tools they need to perceive the unseen messages permeating a system of injustices for what they are: a reminder to look at things as though they can be otherwise, as inspiration and courage to release imagination (Greene 1995). Maxine Greene writes, "It may be the recovery of imagination that lessens the social paralysis we see around us and restores the sense that something can be done in the name of what is decent and humane" (1995, 35). This is possible when children maintain an emotional connection to what Mary Warnock calls "the infinity or inexhaustibleness of things" (1976, 207) because that is what invites them to create and share their own meaning. If the world is truly inexhaustible, there is room for all our stories. And by making room for them all, we create opportunity to find the connections between them all. Six-year-old Evelyn explained it this way: "Hearing other people's ideas helped me to feel visible again."

Story Sharing Is a Process of Authoring Authors

A long-term project of teacher research helped Karen Gallas see for herself the process Evelyn describes as she documented her experiences alongside children during sharing time. Through the research, she came to make an important distinction between *author* and *authoring*. In making a story public during story sharing, the act of authoring positions the teller of the story to learn from the telling. Gallas writes: "Authoring represents a physical incarnation of imagination as it comes in contact with the world. It is distinguished from more internal, imaginative processes (for example, reverie and fantasy) because it is a public event in which an individual presents an original text to an audience" (2001, 477). Even though the author brings a product—a story—to share, it is this act of authoring that is the focus and intent of story sharing. Woodson describes the effect: "Writing taught me everything I know about creating worlds where

people could be seen and heard. Where their experiences could be legitimized. And where my story read or heard by another person inspired something in them that became a connection between us. A conversation. And isn't that what this is all about—finding a way at the end of the day to not feel alone in this world, and a way to feel like we've changed it before we leave?" (2019)

Children experience the world we prepare for them. It's our job to draw out the tools of knowing and meaning making and creating that every child is equipped with and create the conditions in which they will reach toward a community of others who are reaching toward them. It is a space of belonging and common humanity and imagination where we experience difference as opportunity to find connection—and to find the joy that exists when we do. Children, alongside adults, are trying to make sense of the world, and in the stories they tell, in the ways that they interact with each other and with their environment, and in the ways that they respond to questions we don't know the answers to ourselves, there are invitations for our own imagination to join in.

Materials Exploration: Clarifying Your Teacher Research Questions

- **Materials needed:** Gather large paper to use as a placemat, drawing paper to work on, and oil pastels. You'll also need your journal and favorite pen for writing.

- **Getting ready:** Set up your oil pastels in an environment with careful attention to creating a space without distractions. For this materials experience, I want to invite you to reflect back across the book and consider the entire structure of story workshop: preparation, provocation, invitation and negotiation, creation, and sharing.

- **Play:** Use these materials to map your theory of how this structure supports young learners.

- **Reflect:** After at least fifteen uninterrupted minutes of mapping your theory, turn to your journal. Through writing, reflect on what arose as a part of this structure that you're finding the most uncertainty around or curiosity about. Use that uncertainty and curiosity to form a question that will guide your teacher research.

Remember to consider questions you are genuinely curious about, questions that you don't already know the answer to or don't have one specific answer to, and questions that leave plenty of room for exploring and researching a tension. Write these questions down and then share them with a colleague.

Action Steps: Enrich Your Story Workshop Practice

- If you are concerned about the diversity reflected in the books in your classroom library, seek resources such as We Need Diverse Books, Teaching Tolerance, or *American Indians in Children's Literature*, for support and inspiration. But also consider how you can include the books (and paintings and sculptures) the children publish alongside the trade books you have.

- If you have found it meaningful to use your three words throughout this book as anchors, return to the list and see if you would change them now. Are there other words you would add to the master list? What happens if you choose three new words? How might you use materials to explore these words and their relationship to story workshop as you interpret it?

- If audio recording and transcribing dialogue seems too daunting a task to take on, try finding a time to listen to recordings without transcribing them. You might listen as you commute or walk your dog or wash dishes! When something really catches your interest, write it down. Explore patterns that emerge over time.

"Our instinct is to
learn how to live."

—Lucius (age 8)

CHAPTER SEVEN
Living and Learning

We try to avoid any pre-definition that obliged you not to play the game of life with the children—[we are] against all pedagogy whose purpose is in some way to predict the result, which is a sort of predictor that pre-determines the result, and that becomes a sort of prison for the child and for the teacher, and for the human being.

—Carlina Rinaldi, *In Dialogue with Reggio Emilia* (2005, 181)

See the Online Resources for a collection of videos (Videos 7.1 and 7.2) that I hope will support your synthesis of all you've read and inspire you to dive into story workshop in your own context.

Video 7.1 From Sneak Peek to Sharing: Children Ages 3–5

Video 7.2 Bringing a New Student into Story Workshop: Children Ages 5–7

See page ix on how to access these videos.

Stories Create Possibility—and Limit It, Too

Story workshop makes use of something children want to do (play with just about anything they can get their hands on) to facilitate practice in something that humans do (use stories to make sense of their lives). In other words, story workshop is an attempt to structure a way to play the game of life with children in school. Like any strategy or structure we implement in our classrooms, it is both a container of story and a story in itself. The way that we approach our work is filled with the beliefs and values and fears and assumptions we already hold. The decisions we make are influenced by the predictions we make, which are always remnants of past experience. The stories we tell ourselves about children and writing and school both expand and contract the imagination we apply toward the creation of experiences and environments as they, in turn, expand and contract the opportunities children have when they are in our care.

In our work with very young children, if we pay attention to who they are instead of who we imagine them to be, or hope they will be, or wish they were—if we are willing to rewrite our own stories about who they are, what they want, what they need, and what they can do—we will notice and wonder new things to inspire and guide our research. This can, in turn, fulfill our own search for meaning.

I'd like to bring this book to an end by sharing a story (not much of a spoiler, I know) that was written by five-year-old Pavi and by sharing what Pavi's story helped me to value as a teacher-researcher trying my best to work in solidarity with children. Now, Pavi was one of those children who had a particularly unique gift of oral language from a very young age. Her abilities to voice her thoughts with words makes her thinking particularly relatable to adults. This story was captured by her teacher while Pavi played and told her story.

Pavi began,

Pavi playing with natural materials

Once upon a time there was a wormy and he was a curious chap. One bright morning he decided to explore. He slid headfirst down a wide slippery log and something prickled his nose. He saw that there was something big and prickly and he looked closer and it was a cactus. He climbed on the big cactus and decided to have a picnic.

At this point she looked up at the teacher and said, "This story is inspired by *Wiggly, Waggly* [a book they'd recently enjoyed together as a class]." She continued,

Then he squirmed off and met a seed.

"I'm Worm," said the worm.

"And I'm a seed," said the seed.

"Hi, Seed."

"Hi, Worm."

Then they were friends. They saw a big slippery something to climb that Worm thought would be nice to climb. "I'm very roly-poly and round," said the seed, "so I think I can't climb it."

Worm said, "Don't worry, little seed. I'll coil my tail around you and pull you up." The worm changed his mind and pushed the seed up with a headstand.

The seed says, "Oopsie, I will fall!"

"Don't worry seed, I will give you an idea so you don't fall."

Pavi looked up again and, with a wink in her voice, clearly aware that the teacher was listening with rapt attention and in on the joke, said, "Sounds like he's a brainy worm." Then she went back to the story.

The worm pushed the seed up the log. Oopsie, they didn't know they were heading straight for a ditch! They fell into the ditch. They were squirming all around. "How will we get out?"

And Pavi said to her teacher, "Imagine being stuck in a ditch. Now comes the happy part, the idea part!"

Then the worm had an idea. He said, "You stay here. I'll go up because I'm a squirmy worm and then I'll find a way to get you out." The worm squirmed up while the seed waited down in the ditch. Seed wasn't lonely; he was happy because he had another seed friend with him. Then the worm turned and saw a big leaf in the foggy mist. All of a sudden something wonderful happened. An idea popped into his mind. He grabbed one end of the leaf and put the other end into the ditch. "Seed, will you hold onto this leaf so I can pull it up and you with it?"

The seed said to the other seed, "Grab on, too!" Up they came. They wondered, "How do we get home?"

Pavi looked up from her story and said to her teacher, "Well, now there's a little bit of an adventure. Do you remember that the worm was a curious chap? Because of all this curiosity, he said, 'I want to try a different way home.'" She looked up at her teacher again. "Perhaps I forgot to tell you that Seed is a scaredy-cat."

> "I'm scared, scared, scared right now."
>
> "I'm scared, too. I want the same way."
>
> So the worm said, "I know you'll be OK with all our friendship."
>
> "OK," said the seeds. The worm gave them a big hug. With all that hugging he also said, "Let's go!" The seeds took a deep breath and started going with the worm. "But don't fall into the ditch again," said the worm with a tremble.
>
> The worm dragged them alone to a cozy spot. They climbed onto a big elephant trunk–like thing. The worm and the seeds were scared because they would fall. . . . How would they get down? Suddenly, the worm had an idea, idea, idea.

Pavi looked up at her teacher, smiled, and said, "This story woke up in my mind from seeing all the teamwork in our classroom." And then she went on to finish her story.

> And so the worm went onto the pine tree he had seen and the seeds wedged in too. The worm went down and slowly, the seeds did, too. They climbed the log and went home, and from then on, the three of them were ever friends.
>
> The end

Pavi exploring the natural world

Pavi's Wisdom for Teacher Researchers

When Something Is Prickly, Look Closer

". . . there was something big and prickly and he looked closer . . ."

Documentation is a powerful strategy that helps us lean in when something confuses or surprises us. But this is not an easy task. Carlina Rinaldi explains why it can be so difficult:

> The real issue in documentation, with which I am trying more and more to struggle, is who is observing and who is observed. And I see a lot of reciprocity. When you take a picture or you make a document, in reality you don't document the child but your knowledge, your concept, your idea. So it's more and more visible—your limits and your vision about the child. You show not who that child is, but your thought. You don't show the child, but the relationship and the quality of your relationship, and the quality of your looking at him or her. That is why it's so dramatic because the king is naked! (2005, 196)

Documentation forces us to question our own assumptions, to wrestle with our own limitations, and to stretch the boundaries of what we thought possible—all while accepting responsibility for what we might not yet know while we determine what to do next. Documentation opens us up to vulnerability, but it also provides us with tools and structures we need to navigate the prickly things we feel while we move through and beyond new territory toward a more genuine relationship with children, with learning, and with our work.

Learn to View Mistakes as Oopsie Moments

"Oopsie, they didn't know they were heading straight for a ditch! They fell into the ditch."

Children arrive in this world without expectation that there should be negative consequences to exploring, making meaning, and testing hypotheses. They are ready to learn to live, but they don't yet know how to stop and think. And they don't yet know what to stop and think about. They make mistakes. Research is the driver of our relationship with the world, and with the people we encounter in the world, helping us find boundaries as we explore the territory. For this reason, where there is research, there is vulnerability. There is simply no way to move through not knowing toward knowing without vulnerability coming along for the ride. To be in a state of wonder is to be vulnerable; to learn is to be vulnerable; to create is to be vulnerable. We are all born to this world naturally curious, seeking connection and belonging to the community we find ourselves a part of. And the world lets us know the answers: Are we worthy? Are we capable? Do the things that concern us matter to the world? Are we loved? When things don't work out as we planned, what does the world have to tell us about who we are and what might happen next?

Ideas Are Wonderful

"Now comes the happy part, the idea part!"

Carlina Rinaldi writes,

> **As human beings, we are all researchers of the meaning of life. Yet it is possible to destroy this attitude of the child with our quick answers and our certainty. How can we support and sustain this attitude of children to construct explanations? How can we cultivate the child's intention to research? (2004, 2)**

I wonder if it is possible to support this attitude in children if we do not value it in ourselves?

Stay Open to Inspiration

"All of a sudden something wonderful happened.
An idea popped into his mind."

When adults are vulnerable and open, it becomes possible for children to be seen and heard with the full force of their own unique vitality. This vitality is one they have a right to translate into action, which happens best when we are willing to make use of our own.

Traditional curriculum scripts rely on and perpetuate stereotypes of children and childhood by reinforcing generalities and often limitations. But these scripts also limit the teacher's rights to translate their ideas, their feelings, their observations, and their questions into action. When scripted curriculum shows up in the context of high-stakes testing and high-risk consequences, it further constrains our capacity to do so. As Jerome Bruner cautioned, our capacity for the playful and curious attitude required for learning is curtailed when there is too much consequence. If we are to create opportunities for children to control their own stories, we must find ways to inspire their courage to become more as themselves. To do this, we must be more as ourselves.

Children know about relationship. They need it for their very survival. When we enter the classroom with predetermined scripts and certainty about what will happen, we make it difficult for children to be more as themselves because they understand that teachers use those scripts to hide who they are as well.

Appreciate Adventure

"Well, now there's a little bit of an adventure."

We cannot be the delivery mechanism for lines other people have written for us—whether that someone is Piaget or Montessori or Malaguzzi or Pearson or Graves. We must, instead, reconceptualize ourselves as researchers, even if our own attitudes of research were destroyed as children. How do we find and rekindle our own curiosity?

Remember the Power of Teamwork

"So the worm said, "I know you'll be OK with all our friendship."

Remember that children are ready to help us, and they are born willing. Like Pavi, all children have powerful forms of wisdom to share with us that we have very likely long forgotten. They want us by their side because they know that we also hold wisdom, expertise, experience, and access to a wealth of resources that they need and want and that we can make available to them. We all come into the world imperfect—hardwired to struggle, primed to explore and blunder and resolve to keep going. If we want to support habits of persistence and resilience, we have to learn to trust and value the struggle in solidarity with children.

Joy Is a Result of Challenge and Struggle

Pavi has a particular gift for using words that give us a window into the kinds of active world-making we all do all our lives, or at least that we are capable of doing from the beginning. Her use of metaphor gives us a powerful glimpse into the way children see the world—not just this child but all children. In an interview with NPR's Scott Simon, author C Pam Zhang said, "I think we have to expand our definition of writing. I've taken to saying in recent years that walking is writing. Crying is writing. Talking to your friend is writing. All these experiences help you give a shape to what you're thinking about the world, and that will come back to the page eventually" (Zhang 2020). Was Pavi writing? I think so. Not only was she writing an engaging story, but she was writing her way into possibility and a making of a world she wanted to see and participate in. It was reflective of the world being written by the experiences she had in school. She was writing her teacher in, too. And in reading her story, we can learn to read the world in new ways, to imagine our participation in it with more possibility, more connection, more delight, more beauty. We can write *ourselves* into Pavi's story.

Children willingly place themselves in the position of struggle and disequilibrium. This is hard work. It is the work of freedom. In her book, *We Want to do More than Survive: Abolitionist Teaching and the Pursuit of Educational Freedom,* Bettina Love quotes Michael Hames-García: "The very fact of freedom's incompleteness (no one is free so long as others remain unfree) necessitates action directed at changing society. Freedom, therefore, is ultimately a practice, rather than a possession or a state of being" (2019, 9). We can support, encourage, inspire, and challenge in service of this practice, or we can shut it down with certainties, easy answers, judgment, and our own fear of not knowing how to engage in this practice well or right or even adequately. There is so much power in an adult who is willing (like Worm) to offer a hand up toward the unknown. This kind of relationship and collaboration is the wellspring of joy. I am not talking about "the type of fabricated and forced joy found in a Pepsi commercial; I am talking about joy that originates in resistance, joy that is discovered in making a way out of no way, joy that is uncovered when you know how to love yourself and others, joy that comes from releasing pain, joy that is generated in music and art that puts words and/or images to your life's greatest challenges and pleasures, and joy in teaching from a place of resistance, agitation, purpose, justice, love, and mattering" (Love 2019, 15).

It is difficult for anyone but especially adults to remember that it is precisely at the moment that we are willing to feel most vulnerable that we are primed to do the most learning. Curiosity has healing power—it can soothe the discomfort of vulnerability. Curiosity can make us comfortable with uncertainty. The world is an uncertain place and play is the strategy we have that makes it possible for us to thrive; play invites a welcoming attitude toward change

and makes not knowing less dangerous. Play makes learning less dangerous.

We need to ask ourselves not only what supports children to be seen and heard but also what at the same time communicates to children that they are *worthy* of being seen and heard. What kind of practices ensure that each child walks into the classroom each day knowing that they matter? That the work that goes on there each day couldn't happen without them—that it wouldn't be the same without them? We can ensure children learn how to live like they matter, and in so doing, explore what it feels like for ourselves. We can practice. We can write a new story. We can fulfill our commitment to offer joy, not to protect us from the hard stuff, but to find out what it means to move through it together.

WORKS CITED

Ayers, William. 2019. "I Shall Create! Teaching Toward Freedom." In *Teaching When the World Is on Fire*, edited by Lisa Delpit, 3–15. New York: The New Press.

Barazzoni, Renzo. 2000. *Brick by Brick: The History of the "XXV Aprile" People's Nursery School of Villa Cella*. Reggio Emilia, Italy: Reggio Children.

Barrett, Lisa Feldman. 2017a. "Poverty on the Brain." *Thrive Global*, June 8. https://medium.com/thrive-global/neuroscience-reveals-that-growing-up-poor-changes-the-mind-fcf424ea9f33.

———. 2017b. "You Aren't at the Mercy of Your Emotions—Your Brain Creates Them." TED video, 18:28. Filmed December 2017 in San Francisco. www.ted.com/talks/lisa_feldman_barrett_you_aren_t_at_the_mercy_of_your_emotions_your_brain_creates_them?language=en.

———. 2018. *How Emotions Are Made: The Secret Life of the Brain*. New York: Mariner Books.

Bateson, Gregory. 2002. *Mind and Nature: A Necessary Unity*. Cresskill: Hampton.

Bishop, Rudine Sims. 2015. "Mirrors, Windows, and Sliding Glass Doors." Reading Rockets. www.readingrockets.org/sites/default/files/Mirrors-Windows-and-Sliding-Glass-Doors.pdf.

Brown, Brené. 2018. *Dare to Lead: Brave Work. Tough Conversations. Whole Hearts*. London: Vermilion.

Bruner, Jerome. 1986. *Acutal Minds, Possible Worlds*. Cambridge, MA: Harvard University Press.

Caine, Renate Nummela, and Geoffrey Caine. 1997. *Unleashing the Power of Perceptual Change: The Potential of Brain-Based Teaching*. Alexandria, VA: Association for Supervision and Curriculum Development.

Cambourne, Brian. 2015a. "Is It Possible to Apply the Basic Principle of 'Emulating Nature's Best Biological Ideas to Solve a Human Problem' to an Area of the Social Sciences, (in This Case Learning to Read)?" *Cambourne's Conditions of Learning: An Ecologically Valid and Educationally Relevant Theory of Literacy Learning* (blog), September 2. www.cambournesconditionsoflearning.com.au/conditions-of-learning-blog-spot/is-it-possible-to-apply-the-basic-principle-of-emulating-natures-best-biological-ideas-to-solve-a-human-problem-to-an-area-of-the-social-sciences-in-this-case-learning-to-read.

———. 2015b. "What Does a 'Biological Perspective for Addressing the Problem of Learning to Read' Look Like?" *Cambourne's Conditions of Learning: An Ecologically Valid and Educationally Relevant Theory of Literacy Learning* (blog), October 2. www.cambournesconditionsoflearning.com.au/conditions-of-learning-blog-spot/what-does-a-biological-perspective-for-addressing-the-problem-of-learning-to-read-look-like.

Center on the Developing Child at Harvard University. n.d. "Key Concepts: Brain Architecture." https://developingchild.harvard.edu/science/key-concepts/brain-architecture/.

Chakrabarti, Meghna, Prudence Carter, and Ibram X. Kendi. 2019. "Part I: Achievement Gap, or Opportunity Gap? What's Stopping Student Success." *On Point*, September 9. Boston, MA: WBUR and NPR. www.wbur.org/onpoint/2019/09/09/achievement-gap-opportunity-education-schools-students-teachers.

Cobb, Edith. 1993. *The Ecology of Imagination in Childhood*. New York: Columbia University Press.

Csikszentmihalyi, Mihaly. 2008. *Flow: The Psychology of Optimal Experience*. New York: Harper Row.

Dyson, Anne Haas. 1990. "Symbol Makers, Symbol Weavers: How Children Link Play, Pictures, and Print." *Young Children* 45 (2): 50–57.

Dyson, Anne Haas, and Celia Genishi, eds. 1994. *The Need for Story: Cultural Diversity in Classroom and Community*. New York: Teachers College Press.

Eberhardt, Jennifer L. 2020. *Biased: Uncovering the Hidden Prejudice That Shapes What We See, Think, and Do*. New York: Penguin Books.

Edwards, Carolyn, Lella Gandini, and George Forman, eds. 2012. *The Hundred Languages of Children: The Reggio Emilia Experience in Transformation*. Santa Barbara: ABC-CLIO.

Edwards, Carolyn, Lella Gandini, and John Nimmo. 2015. *Loris Malaguzzi and the Teachers: Dialogues on Collaboration and Conflict among Children, Reggio Emilia 1990*. Lincoln, NE: Zea E-Books. 29. https://digitalcommons.unl.edu/zeabook/29.

Eisner, Elliot W. 2002. *The Arts and the Creation of Mind*. New Haven, CT: Yale University Press.

Eisner, Elliot. 2006. "The Satisfactions of Teaching." *Educational Leadership* 63 (6): 44–46.

Freire, Paulo. 1997. *Pedagogy of the Oppressed*. New York: Continuum.

Gallas, Karen. 2001. "'Look, Karen, I'm Running Like Jell-O': Imagination as a Question, a Topic, a Tool for Literacy Research and Learning." *Research in the Teaching of English* 35 (4): 457–92.

———. 2003. *Imagination and Literacy: A Teacher's Search for the Heart of Learning*. New York: Teachers College Press.

Oliver, Mary. n.d. "Wild Geese." Read by the author. On Being Studios at Soundcloud. https://soundcloud.com/onbeing/wild-geese-by-mary-oliver.

Ginsburg, Kenneth R. 2007. "The Importance of Play in Promoting Healthy Child Development and Maintaining Strong Parent-Child Bonds." *American Academy of Pediatrics* 119 (1): 182–91. https://pediatrics.aappublications.org/content/119/1/182.

Graves, Donald H. 2003. *Writing: Teachers and Children at Work*. Portsmouth, NH: Heinemann.

Graves, Donald, and Virginia Stuart. 1985. *Write from the Start: Tapping Your Child's Natural Writing Ability*. New York: E. P. Dutton.

Gray, Peter. 2011. "The Decline of Play and the Rise of Psychopathology in Children and Adolescents." *American Journal of Play* 3 (4): 443–63. www.journalofplay.org/sites/www.journalofplay.org/files/pdf-articles/3-4-article-gray-decline-of-play.pdf.

Greene, Maxine. 1995. *Releasing the Imagination: Essays on Education, the Arts, and Social Change*. San Francisco: Jossey-Bass.

Haidt, Jonathan, and Greg Lukianoff. 2018. "How to Play Our Way to a Better Democracy." *The New York Times*, September 1. www.nytimes.com/2018/09/01/opinion/sunday/democracy-play-mccain.html.

Hammond, Zaretta. 2015. *Culturally Responsive Teaching and the Brain: Promoting Authentic Engagement and Rigor Among Culturally and Linguistically Diverse Students*. Thousand Oaks, CA: Corwin.

Heath, Chip, and Dan Heath. 2007. *Made to Stick: Why Some Ideas Survive and Others Die*. New York: Random House.

Holmes, Jamie. 2016. *Nonsense: The Power of Not Knowing*. New York: Random House.

hooks, bell. 2018. *All About Love: New Visions*. New York: William Morrow.

Horowitz, Alexandra. 2013. *On Looking: About Everything There Is to See*. London: Simon and Schuster.

Huyck, David, and Sarah Park Dahlen. 2019. "Diversity in Children's Books 2018" (infographic). *Sarah Park Dahlen, Ph.D.* (blog), June 19. Created in consultation with Edith Campbell, Molly Beth Griffin, K. T. Horning, Debbie Reese, Ebony Elizabeth Thomas, and Madeline Tyner, with statistics compiled by the Cooperative Children's Book Center, School of Education, University of Wisconsin–Madison: https://ccbc.education.wisc.edu/literature-resources/ccbc-diversity-statistics/books-by-about-poc-fnn/. Retrieved from https://readingspark.wordpress.com/2019/06/19/picture-this-diversity-in-childrens-books-2018-infographic/.

Immordino-Yang, Mary Helen. 2016. *Emotions, Learning, and the Brain: Exploring the Educational Implications of Affective Neuroscience*. New York: W. W. Norton.

Jabr, Ferris. 2019. "The Story of Storytelling." *Harper's Magazine*, March. https://harpers.org/archive/2019/03/the-story-of-storytelling/.

Jiwa, Bernadette. 2018. *Story Driven: You Don't Need to Compete When You Know Who You Are*. Australia: Perceptive Press.

Lazar, Althier M., Patricia A. Edwards, and Gwendolyn Thompson McMillon. 2012. *Bridging Literacy and Equity: The Essential Guide to Social Equity Teaching*. New York: Teachers College Press.

Le Guin, Ursula K. 2004. *The Wave in the Mind: Talks and Essays on the Writer, the Reader, and the Imagination*. Boston: Shambhala.

Lewis, Sarah. 2014. *The Rise: Creativity, the Gift of Failure, and the Search for Mastery*. New York: Simon and Schuster.

Lonergan, Kenneth. 2003. "In Times Like These." *The New York Times*, February 23. www.nytimes.com/2003/02/23/theater/spring-theater-in-times -like-these.html.

Lotto, Beau. 2017. *Deviate: The Science of Seeing Differently*. New York: Hachette Books.

Love, Bettina. 2019. *We Want to Do More Than Survive: Abolitionist Teaching and the Pursuit of Educational Freedom*. Boston: Beacon Press.

MacKay, Susan Harris. 2002. "The Research Mind Is Really the Teaching Mind at Its Best: An Interview with Karen Gallas." In *Language Development: A Reader for Teachers,* edited by Brenda Miller Power and Ruth Shagoury Hubbard, 139–51. New Jersey: Merrill Prentice Hall.

McNiff, Shaun. 1993. Foreword to *The Ecology of Imagination in Childhood*, by Edith Cobb. New York: Columbia University Press.

Mikkelsen, Nina. 1990. "Toward Greater Equity in Literacy Education: Story-making and Non-Mainstream Students." *Language Arts* 67 (6): 556–66.

Minchin, Tim. 2013. *Roald Dahl's Matilda the Musical*. MP3. New York: Broadway Records/Yellow Sound Label.

Moss, Peter. 2014. *Transformative Change and Real Utopias in Early Childhood Education: A Story of Democracy, Experimentation and Potentiality*. London: Routledge.

Nachmanovitch, Stephen. 1990. *Free Play: Improvisation in Life and the Art*. New York: Putnam.

Newkirk, Thomas. 2014. *Minds Made for Stories: How We Really Read and Write Informational and Persuasive Texts*. Portsmouth, NH: Heinemann.

Paley, Vivian Gussin. 1979. *White Teacher*. Cambridge: Harvard University Press.

———. 1986. "On Listening to What the Children Say." *Harvard Educational Review* 56 (2): 122–31.

———. 2004. "The Classroom as Narrative." *Schools: Studies in Education* 1 (2): 63–74. www.jstor.org/stable/10.1086/589211.

Popova, Maria. 2017. "How to Know Everything About Everything: Laura Riding's Extraordinary 1930 Letters to an 8-Year-Old Girl About Being Oneself." *Brain Pickings* (blog), February 27. www.brainpickings.org/2017/02/20/laura-riding-four-unposted-letters-to-catherine/.

———. 2018. "The Building Blocks of Personhood: Oliver Sacks on Narrative as the Pillar of Identity." *Brain Pickings* (blog), January 13. www.brainpickings.org/2018/01/15/oliver-sacks-identity-self-narrative/.

Reese, Debbie. 2019. "An Indigenous Critique of Whiteness in Children's Literature." *Children and Libraries* Digital Supplement, August. https://journals.ala.org/index.php/cal/article/view/7101/9662.

Rinaldi, Carlina. 2004. "The Relationship Between Documentation and Assessment." *Innovations in Early Education: The International Reggio Exchange* 11 (1): 1–4.

———. 2005. *In Dialogue with Reggio Emilia: Listening, Researching and Learning*. New York: Routledge.

Rosen, Harold. 1986. "The Importance of Story." *Language Arts* 63 (3): 226–37.

Rothschild, Amy. 2017. "Is America Holding Out on Protecting Children's Rights?" *The Atlantic*, May 2. www.theatlantic.com/education/archive/2017/05/holding-out-on-childrens-rights/524652/.

Scarry, Elaine. 2011. *On Beauty and Being Just*. London: Duckworth.

Solnit, Rebecca. 2014. *The Faraway Nearby*. London: Granta Books.

Souto-Manning, Mariana, and Jessica Martell. 2016. *Reading, Writing, and Talk: Inclusive Teaching Strategies for Diverse Learners, K–2*. New York: Teachers College Press.

Thunberg, Greta. 2018. "School Strike for Climate—Save the World by Changing the Rules." TEDx video, 11:10. Filmed November 2018 in Stockholm, Sweden. www.ted.com/talks/greta_thunberg_school_strike_for_climate_save_the_world_by_changing_the_rules/transcript?language=en.

Tversky, Barbara. 2019. *Mind in Motion: How Action Shapes Thought*. New York: Basic Books.

Warnock, Mary. 1976. *Imagination*. London: Faber.

Whyte, David. 2019. "David Whyte: The Conversational Nature of Reality." Transcript of interview by Krista Tippett. *On Being*, December 12. https://onbeing.org/programs/david-whyte-the-conversational-nature-of-reality/.

Wilson, Edward O. 2018. *The Origins of Creativity*. New York: Liveright.

Woodson, Jacqueline. 2019. "What Reading Slowly Taught Me About Writing." TED video, 10:47. Filmed April 2019 in Vancouver, British Columbia. www.ted.com/talks/jacqueline_woodson_what_reading_slowly_taught_me_about_writing.

Zhang, C Pam. 2020. "Into the West, from the Far East: 'How Much of These Hills Is Gold.'" Transcript of interview by Scott Simon. *Weekend Edition Saturday*, April 4. www.npr.org/2020/04/04/827241624/into-the-west-from-the-far-east-how-much-of-these-hills-is-gold.